THE EMPTY VOICE

THE EMPTY VOICE

Acting Opera

LEON MAJOR
with MICHAEL LAING

AMADEUS
PRESS

AN IMPRINT OF HAL LEONARD CORPORATION

Published in 2011 by Amadeus Press
An Imprint of Hal Leonard Corporation
7777 West Bluemound Road
Milwaukee, WI 53213

Trade Book Division Editorial Offices
33 Plymouth St., Montclair, NJ 07042

Grateful acknowledgment is made to the following for permission to reprint excerpts of opera libretto translations:

Leyerle Publications, for *L'Italiana in Algeri:* Castel, Nico. *Italian Belcanto Opera Libretti, Volume II.* Geneseo, NY: Leyerle Publications, 2001. Edited by Marcie Stapp.

Colin Ridler, for *L'incoronazione di Poppea:* Monteverdi, Claudio. *The Operas of Monteverdi,* (English National Opera Guides, 45). London: Oneworld Classics, 1992. Edited by Nicholas John, translated by Anne Ridler.

William Weaver, for *La traviata* and *Falstaff:* Verdi, Giuseppe. *Seven Verdi Librettos.* New York: W. W. Norton & Co., 1977. English translations copyright © 1975, 1963 by William Weaver.

The author also gratefully acknowledges the assistance of Dominic Cossa for the translation of *Don Pasquale* and Olga Haldey for the translation of *Eugene Onegin.*

Every reasonable effort has been made to contact copyright holders and secure permission. Any omissions brought to our attention will be remedied in future editions.

Printed in the United States of America

Book design by Michael Kellner

Library of Congress Cataloging-in-Publication Data is available upon request.

ISBN 978-1-57467-195-7

www.amadeuspress.com

For Judith
and our children (though now grown with children of their own),
Joshua, Rebecca, Rachel, and Naomi,
who were (and are) the best supporters, critics, and encouragers
anyone could ever have

MICHAEL LAING, my colleague and friend, was the perfect collaborator. Because he was not of the opera world, he took nothing for granted and demanded, nay, forced me to question my long-held assumptions about theater and opera. We argued and challenged each other in a most fruitful way. Michael died suddenly in the winter of 2010. I shall miss his intellect, his endless probing, his literary advice, his honesty, and, above all, his friendship.

CONTENTS

PREFACE

OPERA IS A SINGER'S MEDIUM, but it comes to life in the theater. Composers write complex and detailed musical scores for stories of passion and conflict, loss and recovery, suffering and joy, forgiveness and despair. Acting is therefore crucial to the experience audiences have in the theater.

Since the early 1990s opera has enjoyed great growth in North America. One reason is that, thanks to supertitles, audiences can now more easily follow the dialogue and the story. Therefore we expect more from singers than just great voices: we expect them to be able to convey the characters they are singing. Without character, singers' voices are empty, however beautiful they may be.

This book will help singers find the dramatic action in key scenes from various operas so that they can fill their voices with character. When singers study a libretto for acting clues as well as the score for musical clues, they not only gain greater insight into their roles, but they have a better understanding of the music as well. Together, musical and acting clues provide the foundation for creating character on the stage. Singers who have that foundation are more relaxed, more focused, and able to sing better. They can perform better together to realize the work dramatically for an audience.

INTRODUCTION

M ANY YEARS AGO I was to direct a new production of *Tosca*, and this was our first rehearsal. It was ten o'clock in the morning, still cool in the hall. Since it was a new production, expectations were high. The entire cast was present, excited yet watchful. Conversations flared up and died down. Only one person was missing: the singer who was to play the lead, Tosca herself. We waited fifteen minutes and then began.

Twenty minutes past the hour she made her entrance. She looked magnificent: high heels, mink coat, elaborate coiffure, pearls. She entered the hall as if she owned it, eyes flickering over the group, making sure we knew she was, as the libretto described her character, "a celebrated singer." My heart sank: this looked like trouble!

At the break we sat down apart from the others to talk about the role. "How do you see Tosca?," she said, looking at me intently. I felt foolish about my doubts: clearly she was just dressed that way to make an entrance, clearly she was a professional who was eager to share ideas. I relaxed and gave what I thought was a pithy analysis of the character. We had a chance to look for some fresh approaches to this powerful but slightly shopworn piece, and I was pleased that she seemed interested in developing them together

I finished. There was a pause. "I don't agree," she said. "That is not the way I do it!"

And it wasn't. About four days into rehearsal we were preparing the first scene between Tosca and her lover, the artist Mario Cavaradossi. There is a moment when Tosca, jealous as she looks at the picture of the woman her lover is painting—a blonde Madonna—says, "Ma falle gli occhi neri!" (But let her eyes be black!). Our Tosca accompanied the line with gestures to convey, as she thought, the singer's intense yet playful nature: she leaned forward, pointed with the index finger of each hand to her eyes, and smiled coyly. It was a gesture made only for effect; it gave no real message to Cavaradossi; and it was fake. I suggested as much, trying to give the point some impact. She stared at me for a moment, then finished the rehearsal and left for the day.

In fact she left for five days, claiming illness. We had begun with two and a half weeks to mount the opera. Taking away time for technical and orchestral rehearsals, what was left was about twelve days at best, seventy-two hours for the principals, of which twenty-four had already been used up. At that point none of the scenes with Scarpia had been prepared. Since Scarpia is Tosca's nemesis, as she is his, they have some of the opera's most intensely dramatic moments. Or should have had: it is not possible to prepare a two-person scene with only one person present.

What resulted was a static and cliché-driven production. The design was serviceable, the lighting appropriate, and the music well played. But, with some honorable exceptions, the singers imitated other singers or simply fell back on stock gestures. There was little interaction between them, and thus there was no conflict, no tension, no drama. The thing was a bore. Our Tosca's statement, "That is not the way I do it," had set the standard for "the way it's done."

The failure was not really her fault. What was to be blamed, apart from my own callowness, was a tradition of opera performance that has grown up over many years and that, in spite of some encouraging signs, persists. According to this tradition, opera is only voice. It's enough for singers to move about the stage gorgeously costumed, appearing and disappearing in magnificent sets, if only the sound is right. Beyond sketching the broad outlines of a character, they do not have to act; the audience has come to listen to them and look at the sets and costumes; perhaps, if all goes well, to be thrilled by an aria, charmed by a duet or a bit of decor.

Which is why we still get productions like the following two reviewed in the *New York Times*, reviews that show the tradition to be in good health. The first piece appeared ten years after the second, in late 2007. How little has changed!

> Several styles are honored here. One is upscale late-18th-century decoration. The other . . . generic, arm-waving swoons and staggers of 19th-century theatricality. Monday's performance . . . seemed not so much to revive an earlier time as to embalm it.

> Opera acting is always a problem, but seldom has it so clearly crossed the line into caricature. Thursday's procession of off-the-shelf gestures included violent shudders, frequent staggering, hand-wringing, wife-flinging, sword-wiggling, and heroine-crawling.

As drama, it was hard to take this . . . seriously. Thank God for the voices.

But in the theater the voices are *not* everything.

Without character, without signs that singers are portraying specific dramatic characters other than themselves, singers' voices can only be empty. They may sound lovely, even powerful or moving, but what audiences are being given is merely a costumed concert, not a living and dramatic performance—sound and fury, signifying nothing. But opera is a theatrical event, not a recital.

I've called this book *The Empty Voice* to stress the point. It echoes Peter Brook's brilliant book of the late 1960s, *The Empty Space: A Book about the Theatre: Deadly, Holy, Rough, Immediate.* He begins with an image of great simplicity and power:

> I can take any empty space and call it a bare stage. A man walks across this empty space whilst someone else is watching him, and this is all that is needed for an act of theatre to be engaged.

This empty space, he sees, is a space waiting to be filled, and he imagines filling it in the clearest, most direct way. That is the positive. Too often, however, that space is overstuffed: as a result, too much theater lacks power and immediacy. In his terms, it is empty. That is the negative. In spite of elaborate sets and striking costumes, there is nothing really there, no substance, no human truth. His book is a diagnosis of why productions are empty and an invitation, in very practical terms, to fill the space of the theater in ways that have both substance and truth.

It is my experience that singers *want* to fill their voices with internal life and authenticity, with character, but that they often do not know how. In this book I propose some ways in which they can do so.

The librettos that composers set to music are stories of human drama. If these stories are not performed in a way that convinces the audience that their events and characters are plausible, the librettist, the composer and the composer's music are short-changed. When singers do not work with each other onstage to create a drama, they short-change each other. And finally, when the theatrical aspect of opera is not expressed, the audience is short-changed.

The singer's job is extremely demanding: to be in technical control of the voice and body, count bars, find the music's rhythm as well as the rhythm of the scene, watch for the tempo from a conductor sometimes barely visible in the pit, find a pitch, manage complex phrasings, express an emotion without tensing the voice, execute a musical style, execute an acting style, sometimes dance or fight, understand and enunciate words (often in a foreign language) clearly, project both music and words to everyone in the house—and all without making it look hard. In addition the singer must understand the character one is playing, work out relationships with other characters on the stage, and react to those other characters. It is a formidable task. No wonder singers fall back on stock gestures.

There are tools available, however, the same tools that actors use to help them create character—tools that can help singers work with each other to realize a play.

The theatrical situation, which actors and singers have in common, is the playing together that realizes the work for an audience. I have found in practice that, when singers study a libretto for clues to the acting as well as the music, they not only gain greater insight into their characters, but they get a better understanding of the music as well. Together, musical and acting clues provide the foundation for creating characters on the stage. Singers who have that foundation, I have discovered, are more relaxed, more focused, and able to sing better.

To be sure, it would be desirable if there were always six weeks for rehearsals. Then singers and director could explore together the nuances of music and text and patiently build a true ensemble, and audiences could experience a more fully realized work of art. But the economics of opera production make this all but impossible. What is possible, however, is for singers to come to a production with confidence in their ability to create character as well as to sing. It is possible for them to not to have to rely on "the way it's done" to survive. And it is certain that, if they have good acting skills, singers can give more to their audiences than just their voices.

Because of supertitles audiences can easily follow the dialogue being sung on the stage; they no longer have to guess what is going on or rustle through their programs. The words are now available, along with the music, to carry the drama. Because audiences know what's happening, they are better able to experience operas as theatrical events, not just musical ones. And that means they are becoming more discriminating about how operas are brought to life in the theater—more discriminating, and more demanding.

What this book presents are some ideas and an array of examples to show how singers can use actors' tools to enrich their performances, to bring more believable and powerful performances to audiences, and to let opera more fully deploy its great theatrical force.

■ ■ ■

Some caveats. Acting in opera can be approached from several directions, and what is presented in this book is only one. There is no discussion of techniques for relaxation or concentration, of theories of breathing or body movement, no exercises for improvisation or for using emotional memory. Other books offer help in these areas. It does not provide material for each voice range or category in the scene studies, nor does it have operatic scenes from the full range of periods, composers, or genres. As well, since I am neither an opera scholar nor a musicologist, I offer no history of opera itself, nor any analysis of performances of particular operas, nor a study of changing musical or performance styles.

What I am is a director. It is my job to define an approach to the opera I'm directing, to persuade the singers and production staff to enter that world, and, during the rehearsal period, to establish an atmosphere that is conducive to creativity as well as presenting a production that is coherent and convincing to an audience. That's the perspective from which I offer these scene studies: the full, *theatrical* realization of a complex work of musical theater.

THE EMPTY VOICE

1

"What Am I Supposed to Do with This Music?" Mozart's *Le nozze di Figaro*, Act II, Scene 1

"IT'S SO LONG," she said, "this introduction. Seventeen bars before I open my mouth. What should I do?"

It was a good question. She was singing her first Countess in *Le nozze di Figaro*, and she was worried about her entrance, the first time the Countess appears in the opera. Seventeen bars may not in fact take a long time to play, but it can seem a lot longer when you're on the stage by yourself with everyone looking at you.

First entrances are important. A character has to establish herself—the audience has to learn who she is and why she is there. The singer has to know why her character is there. This is the first time an audience has seen the Countess, a major role in the opera. Already an entire act has gone by and much has happened, so there is a lot riding on this. Why would Mozart delay the entrance of his heroine for a whole act? Why would he then keep her quiet for seventeen bars?

We should step back. It is the wedding day of Figaro and Susanna, but there are problems. The Count, Figaro's employer, wants to go to bed with Susanna: he will give her a dowry if she gives him her wedding night, his *droit du seigneur*. Figaro is being pursued by Marcellina, the Count's middle-aged housekeeper; he had borrowed money from her, the security being his promise to marry her if he cannot repay it, and Bartolo, the Countess's former guardian, is involved in this plot with Marcellina. Susanna is unhappy to be pursued by the Count; the Countess doesn't like seeing her husband philander; Figaro does not want to marry Marcellina; and he certainly doesn't want Susanna to sleep with the Count. What follows is a series of plots, tricks, and revelations until the right couples end up together: Figaro with Susanna, the Count with the Countess (for the moment), and Marcellina with Bartolo. Love, based on forgiveness, seems to triumph in the end. But not until the end.

A scene from Mozart's The Marriage of Figaro *in a 2010 Glimmerglass Opera Festival production. Front, left to right: Mark Schnaible as the Count and Caitlin Lynch as the Countess; rear, left to right: Patrick Carfizzi as Figaro and Lyubov Petrova as Susanna. (Photo by Claire McAdams)*

That's the general shape of the piece, and it should be basic knowledge for anyone singing in the opera. But to enter her scene, the singer needs more. For that she has to ask some questions. First, *Where am I coming from?* If a character enters a scene without being clear about where her character has been before the scene begins, then she enters the scene ungrounded. All she can do is sing the aria; she will not be able to convey any sense of the character who is singing the aria. Life, for every character, goes on around and behind any particular scene a character is in. Mozart knows this and gives quite clear information to help his singer prepare.

We can see how he does this. In the scene that comes right after this one, Act II, scene 2, we see the Countess picking up a conversation with Susanna that had been interrupted. That conversation would have occurred offstage sometime between the end of Act I and the beginning of Act II. In it she would have heard Susanna telling her about the Count's pursuit of her. That is why, in Act II, scene 2, the Countess asks, "Dunque volle sedurti?" (So he wanted to seduce you?). They're picking up their conversation again. It is in that interrupted conversation that the Countess learned about her husband's desire to seduce Susanna; that's where she is coming from when she steps onstage in Act II, scene 1.

But that is not all the singer has to know. If the Countess is coming from somewhere, she must also be going somewhere. So the singer must ask: *Where am I going?* In this case the answer is easy: she's getting ready for the day and thinking about what she has just heard. And that leads directly to perhaps the most important question: *What do I want?* Every character in every opera steps onstage coming from somewhere, going somewhere, and wanting something; it is knowing what a character wants that gives the singer the reason for being in this place, in this scene, at this moment. The Countess knows exactly what she wants; she says: "Porgi amor, qualche ristoro al mio duolo" (Offer, love, some relief to my ache). She also knows exactly what relief means to her: it means either the return of her beloved or death. What she wants—relief, in one way or another—is her *objective*, her overall aim for the scene. But just knowing what you want—having an objective—does not mean you will reach it, in art or in life. Something prevents the Countess from getting what she wants: the Count is not there. And that is the answer to the next question the singer will have asked: *What is blocking me?* Which leads by iron necessity to the final question, her attempt to find a solution: *How do I overcome this block, this obstacle?* This is the question that poses the challenge: what do I do next? If there is no answer to this question, there is no reason for the Countess to have any further action in the opera; she might as well expire on the spot.

So, as she steps onstage, the Countess has a lot to think about. The results of that thinking are expressed in her aria "Porgi amor." The seventeen bars of the introduction are therefore available for her to do her thinking in and could have been written by Mozart for that very reason. From the thinking she does here, the reason to sing the aria will emerge.

Here is the aria:

Porgi amor qualche ristoro	Offer, love, some relief
Al mio duolo, a' miei sospir.	To my ache, to my sighs;
O mi rendi il mio tesoro,	O return to me my treasure,
O mi lascia almen morir.	Or at least let me die.

No physical action is implied here. Instead, there is intense interior action. The Countess is trying to understand her situation so that she can cope with it. It is her thoughts that are the actions of the scene, and they are just as vivid and real as any physical act. The challenge for the singer is how to make these thoughts evident to an audience.

The aria's music is extraordinarily beautiful; it is a powerful and memorable lament, one of Mozart's greatest. But that can be a problem. If the only reason the aria is there is to be a lament, where do we go once it has been sung? Arias aren't stuck into operas like plums into a pudding; they lead somewhere—to a new action, a new scene. Therefore they have to end differently from the way they began. So the singer has two challenges: what to do during the seventeen-bar introduction, and how to make sure the aria is part of the opera's action and not just a pretty song.

The introduction begins with four chords marked *forte*. They do not tell us what the Countess's thoughts are; rather, they show the strength of her feelings. Still, it is not hard to imagine her thoughts. Since we know, from the first line, that she wants relief from what she cannot bear, what she must be thinking about is what is causing her pain. What the words say is that relief will take one of two forms: either love will bring her loved one back, or it will bring her death. So: after the first *forte* chords, she has sixteen bars to discover what she loves about her husband and why her love is so strong. This discovery is essential: if she does not discover that she still passionately loves the Count, she has no reason to sing the aria. And without the aria and this discovery, there is no reason to have the rest of the opera.

This gives her some possible actions. She may look out of the window and see the Count riding off to a hunt; at once she will have a strong physical image of him to remind her of what she has lost. Or she may find something on her dressing table to remind her of his courtship, not so long ago. Perhaps she picks up a small portrait of him that he gave her when he was pursuing her? She could think what he was like then: the man who wooed her, who disguised himself as a drunken soldier and then as a music teacher, all just to win her. She could remember the look on her guardian's face when he discovered who her suitor really was. (Where do these memories come from? From Beaumarchais's play, *Le barbier de Séville*; this is one way information from outside the opera can be used.) Or perhaps the *forte* chords signal her anger at what she has just learned. If so, she has another kind of challenge: how does she get from being angry at the Count to asking for death if love will not bring her loved one back? Perhaps it's at this point that she sees him outside, riding away, or sees his portrait, or picks up a precious memento. Something has to make her think of the man she has lost rather than the man who has hurt her. With this she is ready to sing the first line of her aria.

In the audience, watching her, we will not know what her thoughts actually are, but we will see that she is thinking. If the singer is committed to her character's internal actions and not just posing, our interest will be aroused and we will be paying attention when she begins to sing— her thoughts will be revealed.

Commitment is key. Many years ago I saw a production of Eugene O'Neill's experimental play *Strange Interlude*, in which the characters speak their own private thoughts aloud even as they are being talked to by other characters—which means that the actual playing time of the production is quite long. I watched this play unfold over almost five hours, and at no time was I bored or uninvolved. The reason was that the actors had committed themselves so completely to playing in this new style that they were able to carry me along as they played. For the first time, I understood the kind of commitment audiences can make if the performers themselves are committed to the drama—and if they have the skill to enact their commitment.

The actions that the Countess chooses will provide the context for her other request, that love should let her die. Does she mean this literally? Or is it simply blurted out in anger and despair? The Countess makes her request—"o mi lascia almen morir"—and says it again in the repeat, turning it over in her mind. On the repeat, there's a crescendo in the orchestra marked to a *forte* on the A-flat; there is also a fermata on the same note in both the orchestra and the vocal part, which gives the moment importance. Does the Countess say the line casually the first time, then muse on the idea of death on the repeated phrase? Is she actually entertaining the idea? She does not start the aria knowing she might to want to commit suicide by the end; she begins it wanting relief from her pain. So it is an idea that comes to her as she feels her way through what she has learned from Susanna. The dynamic of *piano* returns immediately after that and stays for the rest of the aria. She then repeats once more, "o mi lascia almen morir." Why? Is she attracted to the idea of death? Frightened by it? Whatever the answer is will give us two things: first, a reason for the repeats—the dramatic reason that she has to sing them here—and second, information about the Countess. Each appearance she makes after this will be informed by the attitude she takes here, since each moment affects the next. Her wish to die is never mentioned again in the opera. If it were mentioned again, then its meaning in this first aria would be different, and the nature of the aria, and of the Countess's character, would be different.

However, something does happen later in Act II that helps clarify what the Countess wants here, in Act II, scene 1. In Act II, scene 8, seven scenes later, the angry Count discovers that the only person in his wife's dressing room has been Susanna, not Cherubino, whom he had thought the Countess had hidden there; he had suspected she had the same interest in Cherubino that he has in Susanna. He begs the Countess to forgive him, using a term he thinks will be irresistible: for the first time in the opera, he calls her by her name. Her response is significant:

CONTE
Rosina ...

CONTESSA
Crudele! Più quella non sono;
Ma il misero oggetto del vostro
    abbandono
Che avete diletto di far
    disperar.

COUNT
Rosina ...

COUNTESS
Cruel man! No longer am I she,
But the wretched object of your
    neglect,
Whom you have delight in making
    despair.

What the Countess is saying is that she is no longer the Rosina who was once so ardently courted by the Count, just as he is no longer—to her—the ardent lover that he used to be.

This discovery—that she is not now as she once was, that she has changed—can only occur because of the discovery she was in the process of making eight scenes earlier, in "Porgi amor"—that in spite of his betrayal of her, she loves him and wants him back. Perhaps she has changed as much as the Count himself has changed. Discoveries are focal points in dramas. In making this discovery the Countess is seeing that she has a choice to make: she can either give in and accept her role as the injured wife, or she can fight to win him back. She makes her choice, and we can see the effects: something is released in her. She refuses just to suffer and begins to act. The change is not complete in a moment, of course. At first she is a hesitant participant in Figaro's and Susanna's plots. But by Act III she has become the chief plotter. She manages the masquerade that finally exposes her husband and makes him beg her forgiveness. She disguises herself to win him, just as once before he had disguised himself to win her. She controls the timing of the revelations that occur. And then, at the end, she forgives him. So her recognition that she is no longer the woman she once was calls up in her the forces she possessed in the past as Rosina (in the Beaumarchais play), when she plotted as an equal with her lover.

A Countess who sings her aria as a passive creature giving in to despair is difficult to reconcile with the woman, and her actions, revealed over the whole course of the opera. "Porgi amor" reflects her state of mind at the moment she has found out distressing news. It marks the moment that she realizes what she has lost; it is her first encounter with the idea that something may be irretrievably over. This is confirmed and extended when, some twenty-five minutes later in scene 8, she says, "Più quella non sono" (No more am I she). Who would not, in the midst of coming to such a realization, wish for absolutes, either a return to things completely as they were or a way completely out? What her wish for death can show is not the pathos of a victim, but the response of a sensitive woman to a catastrophe in her life. Because of her innate strength, which we learn more and more about as the opera progresses, her full realization in "Porgi amor" of the extent of her loss stimulates her recovery and her attempt to show her husband what he is doing and therefore, if possible, make him change. And it is her emotional depth, as shown in "Porgi amor," that gives her the strength to overcome the barriers, the Count's absence.

The stakes in the second act of Le nozze di Figaro are particularly high. All the characters have their own agendas: Figaro has to find a way to save his marriage and his job; Susanna has to save her virtue and her marriage; the Count has to find a way to get what he wants from Susanna while at the same time keeping his "honor"; and the Countess has to save her marriage and her self-respect. The higher the stakes are, the more intense a scene is: the funnier or the more tragic, and certainly the more dramatic. It is in "Porgi amor" that the stakes for the Countess are made clear: the more intensely she can be shown to understand this, the more vivid and dramatic her character will be. The more vividly she can recall the positive in her life, the more intensely she will wish for an end to her suffering, and the more convincing she will be in bringing her suffering to an end. And her aria will end not in grief, as it began, but in new understanding and resolution.

The introduction to "Porgi amor" can be whatever the singer wants it to be. But whatever her choice, it has to be true to the action of the opera as a whole. As soon as the aria is over, Susanna comes back, and the Countess says, "Vieni, cara Susanna, finiscimi l'istoria" (Come, dear Susanna, tell me the rest of the story). Within minutes, Figaro enters, full of plans to teach the Count a lesson—to dance to a tune that he, Figaro, will provide. So action succeeds action, and the way is open for a vital character to emerge: the Countess, not passive, not merely lamenting beautifully, but full of vitality and determination, a woman fully able to fight for what she wants. Her voice will be full of character, which we in the audience will see and can be excited by.

2

A Little Theory

ALTHOUGH I DO NOT SUBSCRIBE to many theories of acting or directing, some theory in certain instances can be useful. One in particular has shaped many decisions I have made.

The most basic and most powerful theoretical statement I know about the theater comes in those two sentences from Peter Brook's book that I've quoted already in the introduction, but I'm going to quote them again because they are such a useful starting point:

> I can take any empty space and call it a bare stage. A man walks across this empty space whilst someone else is watching him, and this is all that is needed for an act of theatre to be engaged.

It is not easy to imagine talking about opera in these terms. Opera can hardly be thought of as so simple or so spare. From the beginning it was aristocratic, extravagant, virtuosic, grand. Its trajectory was always outward bound, toward high stylization, the play of archetypes, myth.

But the heart of all this, its animating core, is and always has been—paradoxically—something very spare, very simple, and not at all alien to the image Peter Brook evokes. That core is the actions performed by characters who find themselves in conflict with themselves or with other characters over what they want, and who have to discover how to resolve those conflicts, if they can. This is the essence of drama.

We can see what this means by developing the image. The man walking across the empty space is going somewhere. From where? To where? What does he want? Will he get to where he is going? Will someone appear who prevents him? How will the walker deal with this? From the beginning the watcher's attention is engaged (these are, for the moment, his questions) and his attention intensifies as the stakes increase: how important is it that the walker make, or not make, his journey? What is really put at risk by the person trying to prevent him? Perhaps the watcher learns something about the walker that makes him hope he will complete his journey. Perhaps, for other reasons, the watcher wants the impeder to prevail. And so on, and so on. With each new action everything changes, moment by moment like life itself, and so does the watcher's engagement with what he is seeing. And yet the core has not changed: a man walking across an empty space, watched by someone else. In opera it is the same, only the man walking is also singing, the person watching is also listening to music, and the working out of the drama—the action, along with the development of the characters—is being led by that music.

Opera, like all art, is artifice; it is not everyday life. What makes it succeed is craft, the conscious use of skill to make specific choices. The craft in opera, as in any other art, lies in choosing precisely, accurately conceived details, and imaginatively forging them into a whole. The details that are chosen must be specific to the action of the moment, both musically and dramatically. If they are not, if the specific, detailed demands of either music or drama are shirked in favor of generalized attitudes or vague gestures, then the artifice is not sustained, and the performance is incomplete.

The five questions that I proposed in the previous chapter for the singer to ask had a single purpose: to illuminate for her the action of each musical and dramatic moment in the piece. They were intended to help her find the specific, focused details she needed to work with in order to make choices and build up character, and to prepare her to work in rehearsal with her colleagues, the director, and the conductor to make the opera come to life. The same questions must be asked about every character in every scene in every opera.

Answering the questions for each of a singer's scenes is hard work. But it has to be done. Here is an example of what can happen when it is not. I was directing a production of *Rigoletto*. Unexpectedly, we had four weeks to rehearse instead of the more usual two or three; therefore, we had time to work at creating genuine ensemble acting for the production. Or so I thought. At the first rehearsal, the singer playing Marullo made it very clear that all he wanted was to be told where to go on the stage. That was what he understood by the term *action*: what he, the singer, had to do, where he had to go, and how he had to stand, not what his character had to do. His character's name was only a word in a contract. He did not know much about what happened in the rest of the opera; in fact, he did not know much about what was happening even in his own scenes. He knew his music well, *his* music; but because he knew none of the details of the action, he could contribute nothing—as a character—to the action of his scenes. And about all of this he was unapologetic. His obligation, he said, was to bring a trained voice to the production and to move from A to B on the stage as required.

My claim was that he had to know what happened in the rest of the opera so that he could understand why Marullo was in a particular place, and how the character's actions were interwoven with the actions of everyone else so that he could act with them. In the end, this singer did pretty much as he wanted. And the production showed exactly that: a singer whose actions, beyond picking up his cues and hitting his marks, were empty of characterization and had little relation to what any of the other singers were doing.

On top of that, an entirely predictable, entirely avoidable opening-night disaster occurred as a direct consequence of this singer's selfishness. At a certain point in the first scene, Marullo was to take some of the courtiers downstage and sing some lines in conversation with them. Marullo made his move and the courtiers moved with him, but not a sound came from his mouth. He had forgotten his words; he had in, theatrical parlance, "dried." What did the audience see and hear? They saw the movement and heard the chorus, and they heard some music from the pit. The chorus, of course, grew tentative and unsure; as no answers came from the singer, most of them turned to the conductor for help. So what the audience also heard was the maestro singing the words. The audience snickered. It took some time for them to be drawn back into the drama.

Marullo had memorized his moves as he had memorized his notes. But it was all mechanical. So when one part of the mechanism failed, the other parts were at risk. Because he did not understand—or care—why he was moving, or why the other singers were moving with him, he had no means of helping himself. A peril of the empty voice!

My theory about acting in opera is brief and practical. It has two parts, and both have to do with preparation: five questions for singers to ask before they step onstage, and four principles. The five questions you have already seen:

1. Where am I coming from?
2. Where am I going?
3. What do I want?
4. What might block me?
5. How do I overcome that block?

As well, the four principles I believe singers should do before they step onto a stage:

1. Read the opera all the way through.
2. Think about the action.

3. Break down the action of every scene he or she is in.

4. In the case of solo arias, assess who the character is singing to—to self, to God, to another person, to the audience?

If the singer in the *Rigoletto* production had done this preparation, he would have understood who his character was, why he was onstage, and who the characters were with whom he had to interact. Then he would have known what to sing because he would have understood why.

Think about Action

In an opera, as in a play or movie, there must be progress. Action starts with desire, with wanting something. A man and woman love each other. Once they have said, "I love you!," that's it. As an audience, we know where we are, we are set for what comes next: to find out how the lovers go about achieving their love. What has to be done so they can come together? They take steps to achieve their goal. They know what they want and they try to make it come true.

We all want something, but to have drama there must be a barrier. When the man says, "I love you," perhaps the woman says no. Then he has to find a way around this. Why will she not have him? Can he change her mind? Is there a rival? Can he be got rid of? Maybe he really cannot win her; maybe all he can do is go to a foreign country and become rich. Or perhaps she says yes, but her father says no; then the lovers together have to find a way to get around the father and get what they want. Or perhaps she would like to have him, only her family is poor and her mother is ill, so she really should marry the neighbor, who is old and rich but whom she does not love. The variations on this theme are numerous, and in all these cases there are barriers. The actions taken to remove those barriers so that desire can be achieved create their own conflicts. In fact, in the theater as in life, whenever there is desire or anxiety, the primary sources of action, there is conflict.

In the theater, everything depends on conflict. A scene without conflict is not a scene.

He: I love you.
She: I love you.
He: Let's get married.
She: OK.
Both (at altar): I do.

No conflict, no drama, no interest!

Conflicts occur over the course of the story: they occur, they are resolved, then there is a new conflict, followed by a new resolution, and so on. The action progresses until there is some kind of final resolution. Either desire is achieved and fear conquered, in which case there is a coming together (such as a marriage), and the overall form of the piece is that of a comedy; or desire is thwarted and reason to fear is victorious, in which case characters end up alone or dead, and the overall form of the piece is that of a tragedy. Once the final resolution has occurred, there is no more action, and the opera is over.

Action is the source of energy for the drama in opera; it is what gives opera its life and its shape. How the problems are resolved is what makes us, the audience, pay attention. What performers must do is discover the action of a scene: the conflicts and resolutions, the obstacles and the solutions. Finding the actions, external or internal, is the acting process.

But in order to find the actions of the characters they are playing— what they desire or fear, how desires and fears are resolved or moved on from—each singer must understand the plot or action of the entire opera. Once this is understood, the process of character creation can begin.

Read the Opera All the Way Through

The first step in preparing a role is simply to read through the whole score and libretto. In this process, much helpful information will emerge. This will be embedded in what the character has to say and sing, or do, but it can also arise from what other characters have to say about that character, and from how they behave toward him. Does a character inspire fear? Loathing? Desire? In whom? Under what circumstances? Why? Does a character block the aspirations of others? Or is that character the one who is blocked—do others plot against him when he is not onstage?

What characters do when they are not onstage is almost as significant as what they do when they are. Any character in any dramatic piece has a life that an audience assumes continue when he or she is offstage. Singers have the chance to think about this in the read-through. In *Le nozze di Figaro*, for instance, the Countess appears for the first time in Act II, scene 1, and she appears alone. Each of the other main characters appears first with someone else or as part of a larger ensemble; only the Countess has the stage to herself at her first appearance. For her to appear by herself suggests that this is how she is living her life at present—alone. So the first read-through provides basic facts: the setting, the Countess's relationship with her husband, her relationship with her maid Susanna and with Figaro, and so on. It also provides the information that the

Countess knows about her husband's interest in Susanna. But nowhere before her first appearance do we see the Countess learning this. In other words, in order to sing "Porgi amor," the Countess has to know facts that are revealed to the audience only in the following scene, Act II, scene 2. What is suggested in this scene is that the Countess and Susanna were having a conversation before the Countess's entrance. So what the singer learns from the read-through is information that is the raison d'être for her first aria. The Countess brings her offstage life to her first entrance.

Singers approaching a role for the first time must do this kind of read-through. But it's useful for experienced singers as well. This is not to say that they will learn new facts about the action (although they might, particularly in operas as rich as *Le nozze di Figaro* or *Falstaff*); but it is likely that reexamining familiar facts can lead them to understand the action a little differently. The singer who plays Violetta or the Countess at thirty will bring a different view of life to her role than she did at twenty. By contrast, the singer who does not challenge herself but depends instead on "the way it's done" will obviously not give as fresh a performance as the singer who can rediscover her character and therefore recreate her for every production. To repeat a role without fresh investigation, doing it the way it has always been done, leads to performances that are stale and cliché driven and voices that are empty.

Or the director can be bored. When singers will not think about their roles, when all they do is remember "the way it's done," rehearsals can be a nightmare. To deal with this, the director might start introducing elements that he hopes will distract the audience from the uninteresting performance. For example, in Violetta's magnificent aria at the end of Act I of *La traviata*, a hackneyed portrayal can be camouflaged by waiters clearing the table and listening to the character and, perhaps, whispering among themselves. That is not good: it steals the drama from the character, who is at a particularly dramatic point in her development, but it does give the audience something to pay attention to while they are listening to the beautiful aria sung by the beautifully gowned performer whose voice is empty of character or intent.

Or performances can simply be incomprehensible. Once, for a different production of *Tosca*, I noticed that the baritone playing the villain Scarpia moved upstage and stood for a moment with his back to the audience. He then came downstage to look at Tosca. "Why?" I asked him. "Because it's always done that way," he said. "Why?" I asked. He didn't know, and neither did I. With the help of some dramaturges, we found an answer (which may be apocryphal). In the original production, or one very near it, the baritone had suffered from an excess of phlegm, and had found that moment, when the soprano playing Tosca would not be disturbed, to cross upstage and spit. So traditions are born and take hold even though the reasons behind them may have nothing whatever to do with the drama or the action. Where does such an action leave us, the audience? Wondering what is going on, and therefore, perhaps, beginning to lose interest.

In approaching the libretto, whether for the first time or the tenth, it is essential for singers who are not fluent in the language of the libretto to make literal translations of the libretto and find the intentions of the idioms. Thanks to Nico Castel's literal translations, the task is much easier. Singers need the original, they need to know specifically what the librettist put on the page and what the composer responded to in creating the music. They need the clues that images and metaphors in the original language can give about the action and about character.

To translate the other roles is equally important. I am astonished at how often singers translate their own parts but don't really know what their partners are saying. During a rehearsal of *Roméo et Juliette*, I happened to pick up the score of the singer playing Roméo. He was not a French-speaker, so he had dutifully translated his lines. But only *his* lines. At a break, I asked him why he had not translated the other roles.

"Why?" he asked.

"Well," I said, "wouldn't it be useful to know what the other person is saying to you?"

"Why? I wait for my cue, and then I sing. What does it matter if I know or don't know what they're saying? I know what I'm saying."

"So you can have a dialogue," I said. "So you can respond appropriately to what they're saying, or the way they're saying it."

"No," he said; "I know from the markings how to sing. If the marking is *piano*, then I sing *piano*. I do what I'm told."

"But don't you want to know why it's *piano*?"

"No."

His attitude naturally affected Juliette. She had done her translating thoroughly: she knew not only what her lines meant, but what everyone else's meant as well. Therefore she knew why she had to sing what she had to sing, and she did so compellingly. But her scenes with Roméo were agony for her. She got nothing from him. No line had a thought behind it, no line had an intention—frustrating for the singer, irritating for the director, boring for the audience. Without a precise understanding of the dialogue—

the interplay, the give-and-take, all the things that "real" characters do with each other in a play—no interaction, and therefore no genuine drama, were possible.

Punctuation can sometimes give more information than notes and words. Some writers use punctuation to convey information about how the words are to be read. If time is taken to decipher the symbols, often some of the writer's intentions concerning their characters will become clearer. In his libretto for Puccini's *Il tabarro*, for example, Giuseppe Adami uses ellipses, colons, and exclamation marks with great care. I have read this to mean that an ellipsis is a simple transition between thoughts, a movement from thought A to thought B. Colons, on the other hand, show that thought B explains or expands thought A. And an exclamation mark can indicate finality or emphasis.

As singers read through the piece and, if necessary, work on putting it into English, other things will emerge that are also important for building the character. For example, *Le nozze di Figaro* is set in 1785. Its action occurs over the period of a single day: it begins in the morning and ends in the evening. It takes place in various rooms in the castle of Count Almaviva and in the castle garden. What does this say? One thing it says is that the characters live in close proximity, although at the same time they are separated by rigid barriers of class and status. So the risks of being overheard or caught are high. An awareness of this possibility affects how scenes are played. Danger—exposure—can lurk in any corner. And what is more compelling than to watch someone in danger?

Details of setting can stimulate important questions. What was it like to be an aristocrat in the late eighteenth century? What was it like to be a servant in the household of an eighteenth-century aristocrat? What might be helpful to know to begin creating a character who lives in Spain (or France, or Austria) at this period? How would a person of that time walk? Gesture? Hold himself or herself? These and other questions will be answered in detail later in the preparation period and especially in rehearsal. But it is important to start thinking about them early.

Knowledge of the specific details of what actually happens in an opera, then, as well as of where and when the actions occur, form a base from which a character can be built. It is the basis for finding and defining the conflicts in each scene so that later, in rehearsal, these conflicts can be set up and resolved—in a word, acted. A focused and detailed understanding of what happens in the opera, its action, must be part of the preparation. The singer must give it the same attention as he or she gives to musical preparation.

Break Down the Action of Every Scene You Are In

Stanislavski, in *An Actor Prepares*, compares preparing for a role in a play to preparing to eat a large turkey. He notes that most people cannot eat an entire turkey at once, at a single bite. To be able to eat it, we cut it up into halves, quarters, eighths, and finally into bite-sized pieces. So, after the whole opera has been looked at, it must be broken down into smaller pieces. That is the only way to get the basic details of character and action right.

Therefore, the actions of each scene must be broken down. For Act I, scene 1 of *Le nozze di Figaro*, the notes of the singers who are going to play Figaro and Susanna might look like this.

duet
FIG measures room
SUS looks at mirror; is pleased with the hat she has made; asks
   FIGARO if he admires it; repeats this 8 times
FIG continues measuring
SUS demands FIGARO really look at her hat
F/S both appreciate hat made by SUSANNA
recit
FIG measures again
SUS asks why he's measuring
FIG is seeing if bed will fit; says it's a gift from the COUNT, as
   is the room
SUS doesn't want gifts of bed or room; at first won't say why
duet
F/S FIGARO explains why the room is good; SUSANNA drops
   hints as to why the room is bad
FIG begins to be alarmed and suspicious, begs SUSANNA to
   tell more
recit
SUS tells FIGARO to stop fears and suspicions that insult her
FIG begs to hear reasons
SUS explains COUNT's real motives, BASILIO's role,
   COUNT's hope to exercise his *droit du seigneur*
bell
SUS goes to see what COUNTESS wants
FIG finally understands; sings "Se vuol ballare"

That is a lot of work for a scene that might last about five minutes onstage. But, for the singers, writing out these details of action provides very specific information about what happens in it. Then, as the music is learned—its mood, tempo markings, dynamic changes, key changes—specific reference can be made to each part of a scene's action, and the links between music and action can be seen. This will help, too, in understanding the words. As a result, the mechanical tasks of note learning and action breakdown help begin to clarify the intentions of each line and the objectives of each scene—what each character wants at any given moment, as well as what blocks him or her from getting it. Singers have to know this so that we, watching them and listening to them, can know it too.

The idea is that every time characters step onto the stage, we in the audience must learn something about them. The more we know, the more interested we can be.

All the words are important, all of them. I was once invited to watch a rehearsal of Mozart's *Così fan tutte*. *Così* is an opera with many passages of difficult but necessary recitative—necessary because the passages advance the plot and develop the characters. All the singers were struggling to find their meanings so they would know how to play the scenes. But not the director. "Oh, those words don't matter," he said. "Just say them quickly so we can move on to the song."

Now interpretation, the finding of motives and identification of character traits, begins. This is where other kinds of questions begin to be asked. Why does Susanna have to try eight times to get Figaro to look at her bonnet? What is Figaro doing? Is he so busy that he cannot hear her? Or does he choose not to hear her? The approach at this stage should be simply to discover the facts. It should not be to make judgments. If judgments are made in advance about characters, then all that will be noticed, as the libretto is being read, is what supports these judgments. A singer preparing to perform the role of Carmen, for example, might think: "Oh, Carmen is a tramp. Then this is how a tramp walks, this is how she smiles." And, having made this judgment, the singer will then walk like a tramp or smile like a tramp throughout the production, whether it is appropriate at any particular moment or not, in order to justify the judgment. But this obstructs the search for nuances, for what makes Carmen complex, interesting, and therefore worth watching. It leads to a caricature, not a character. A Carmen constructed in this fashion will have no chance to grow and change over the course of the opera, no chance to do what the libretto and music in fact show her doing.

An opera's action occurs moment by moment. Audiences pay attention moment by moment. So the process of creating any performance should also occur moment by moment. Breaking down the action allows singers to find each of those moments. Just as music is prepared phrase by phrase, so characters should be prepared action by action. Unless we have knowledge of a character's past through the libretto, every singer must approach every aria and every line of recitative as a new idea—a new discovery. When Violetta sings "È strano . . ." or the Countess sings "Porgi amor," it must be for the first time. We in the audience can then see the development of the character. It is these new discoveries that help propel the action forward. Characters are built out of the patient accumulation of detail, not out of generalized, vague attitudes. Gestures that have no true relationship to the conflict are generalized and vague. They show no intention, and therefore, in theatrical terms, they are empty. An empty gesture cannot convey anything to the audience.

The presentation of character in a performance onstage will be most convincing if it is an unbroken series of actions. But to create that seamless sense of character, each particular action in each particular scene must first be understood. What follows is a series of scene studies in which I try to show how this small but, I believe, essential bit of theory can help singers prepare for a variety of roles. Each study deals with a particular problem or challenge. No attempt is made to cover every type of role for every kind of voice in every genre of opera. The studies are representative, not inclusive.

3

Acting Action

T HE READ-THROUGH gives the overall action of the opera. Breakdowns give singers the chance to define the particular actions of each scene. The next step is to study how these actions work together dramatically within the scenes. Scene study is the process of finding those specific clues that clarify the actions for each character, playing alone or with others. From this, conflicts are determined.

The core of the scene study process is a set of questions that help clarify what characters want as they prepare to step onto the stage. Knowing that is the only basis from which a singer can enter a scene. It is not enough to know the music, to follow the conductor, to find the marks on the stage. A performer can do all that and still leave the scene dramatically inert, uninteresting to the audience. Uta Hagen's words (from her book *Respect for Acting*) are a reminder of how action drives us forward, but the idea can be found in any contemporary acting book:

> The actions of human beings are governed, more than anything else, by what they want, consciously or unconsciously.

The presentation of character in a performance onstage will be most convincing if it is an unbroken series of actions. But to create that seamless sense of character, each particular action in each particular scene must first be understood.

Action in Monteverdi's *L'incoronazione di Poppea*: Act I, Scene 1, and Act II, Scenes 11–12

In life, as we know, action never ends; it is always one thing after another. But in a work of art there is shape: something begins, develops, and ends. There has to be a shape; otherwise how would people know when to put down the book or leave the theater?

That is the first challenge in this section: to show the shape actions need to have in an opera. What gives action its shape is change: what was expected or hoped for does not occur, unexpected things happen, crises are provoked, and so on. People react; they have to cope. So in this section we will also discuss some theatrical techniques a singer can use for coping with change in a scene, change based either on the discovery of new information or on interactions that provide surprises.

The second challenge is simply the nature of the piece. Monteverdi's *L'incoronazione di Poppea* was first performed more than 360 years ago, in 1642. The conventions of behavior and staging of his time are not ours; they can seem to us strange, and that can be a challenge if we have to prepare to perform with these conventions. However, the strangeness can be managed by exactly the kind of preparation we would use for a modern piece.

The strangeness begins right away, in the prologue. We are in the midst of an argument among three characters. But these are not characters as we might expect from the more naturalistic conventions of novels and plays. In the first place, they have the names of qualities: Fortune, Virtue, and Love. In the second, they appear to be divine. But they are not serene and detached, the way we may think gods should be; instead, they are squabbling over who is most important. The last to speak, the little boy-god Love, is the most combative. He announces that proof of his supremacy is to be demonstrated "oggi" (today). What is to happen in the opera, we infer, is to be his evidence.

It is not easy to see why this should be interesting dramatically—a trio of abstract qualities setting up a test, an opera written to prove a thesis, two goddesses and a little-boy god. How can it be brought to life on a stage?

Yet the drama is there, and we can find it if we can get past our preconceptions. The questions help. First: where are they coming from? That is pretty clear: they are coming from being in the midst of an argument. Where are they going? That is clear as well: they are going to continue arguing until one of them wins. This is the clue we need.

In the prologue, the point is not just that each character represents a different point of view. Rather, it is that each character wants something different. That is where the drama is: in the conflict between characters who want different things. So the prologue is not just an abstract thesis, a disembodied discussion; it is the source of motivation and energy for all the actions to follow. Its conflicts represent on the heavenly plane what is going to happen in the rest of the opera here on Earth. It sets up and dramatizes the question: is Love more powerful than Fortune or Virtue? That is the source of everything that follows.

And it leads to a small but important piece of acting theory. Technically,

Juliana Franco as Poppea in a 2002 Maryland Opera Studio production of The Coronation of Poppea. *(Photo by Stan Barouh)*

these characters—Fortune, Virtue, Love—are personifications, abstract qualities endowed with human characteristics. Nowadays personification is not a mainstream convention. Monteverdi, working with the conventions of his time, was quite comfortable with it. But abstractions and ideas cannot be acted; only their results, the way they are embodied, can be. If a man says to a woman, "I love you," how does she know he is telling the truth? When she hears him, she either wants or doesn't want to believe him. But it is from what she sees him do, his actions, that she knows whether he means what he says. It is the actions that provide, and prove, the idea. We in the audience come to know about characters in the same way: we see what a character does, and therefore we can understand what he or she is thinking or feeling. Feelings are a result of actions. Feelings played in the abstract become generalized—unspecific. No one can play love, or the idea of love; what can be played, however, is an action that is the result of love—a look, a kiss, a movement across the stage.

So we should look for actions that Fortune, Virtue, and Love might perform. We might set the prologue, for example, in some kind of ethereal place with figures conversing as they prune their vines. The beings could wear masks, they could float in the air or descend from the heavens. The vines need not be naturalistic, nor need the figures. The way they prune, the way they move about, the way they interact with each other—their actions—would all give us specific information about them. Because they would each have their own specific objective, because each character would understand where he or she was going, they could show us clearly who they were and what they wanted. And so what might have seemed strange, even perhaps unplayable, is now theatrically interesting.

The action of *L'incoronazione* is complex, full of changes and surprises, most of them tense and ironic, all requiring reactions. Otto, a friend of the emperor Nero, loves Poppea and believes she loves him. But while he has been away she has become Nero's mistress, so naturally she is not interested in Otto any more. The rest of the action works out from that set-up, showing Otto's despair and anger, Poppea's ruthlessness, and Nero's self-absorption. There are appearances by Nero's moralizing tutor, the philosopher Seneca; by Nero's wife, Octavia; and by others. But in the end, Nero and Poppea have their way—they get rid of Seneca, they banish Otto and Octavia—and the little god of Love laughs happily in heaven, having easily won his argument.

Act I, Scene 1— Otto's Return
The first scene is set outside Poppea's palace, at night. Two soldiers of Nero's

guard are sleeping outside the door. Otto enters during the first ritornello. At first he does not see the soldiers.

E pur io torno qui, qual linea al centro	So I return here, as lines to a centre,
Qual foco a sfera e qual ruscello al mare,	As flames to fire's source, or as stream to ocean.
E se ben luce alcuna non m'appare	Though no light's shining to give me greeting,
Ah' so ben io che sta'l mio sol qui dentro	Ah, yet I'm certain that here my love is sleeping.
E pur io torno qui, qual linea al centro.	So I am returning, I turn to her, once more to my centre.

Where is Otto coming from? There is nothing in the score to indicate where he has been, except away from Poppea, and nothing to suggest for how long. There is nothing even to suggest who or what he is, apart from the fact that he loves Poppea and believes she loves him. Given what the opera will show us about her ambition, it is likely he is at least at, or around, her own social level. But is he a soldier? An official? A poet? If there is no information in the opera, we should ask why. There are two possibilities: either Monteverdi thought it did not matter, or he thought his audience would know, since they would have read Tacitus and Suetonius, the Roman historians from whom he and his librettist, Giovanni Francesco Busenello, drew their plot. The latter seems likely: both writers were part of the curriculum for young Venetian men of the period. From them, we learn that Otto was well born and a friend of Nero. They give different information about Poppea: either Otto was already married to her, or he had fallen in love with her while assigned to "protect" her until the emperor could get rid of his wife. This helps, but only a little. Nothing in the opera suggests that Otto and Poppea are or were married. What we do know, because Otto says so, is that, before the opera begins, they had been having a passionate relationship. So what can be said is that Otto is a Roman aristocrat who has been away for a while.

He could be coming from a battle, a foreign posting, his estates in the country, anywhere; the choice that is made will be shown by the singer's specific actions onstage. But what is important is that he has been away far enough and long enough that he does not know that Nero and Poppea are now lovers—and that, from his point of view, enough time has passed for his hopes and desire to intensify, since he is clearly very excited. That is what Monteverdi seems to care about most: Otto's passion. That passion, along with what happens to it, is part of the evidence for Love's case in the prologue.

The next question is: *Where is he going?* For Otto, the answer is pretty clear, and it shows his primary objective, his reason for entering the scene. He is coming back to be with Poppea. That is his overall objective. His *intention*—what he wants at any specific moment—is to get inside Poppea's house. All the similes he uses suggest the strength of his feelings. He compares them to irresistible forces: he is returning "qual linea al centro" (he is thinking of magnetic force), "qual foco a sfera," and "qual ruscello al mare." He cannot help himself. This answers the question: *What does he want?*

He says there is no light to give him greeting. This presents more questions for the singer. Is the lack of light a block? Does Otto think it is a sign he may not get what he wants? Is it only a passing observation? Or is it an early, half-conscious sign that he is unsure about Poppea, or about himself? The next line gives the clue, telling us that whatever Otto may secretly fear, his will and desire are for the moment stronger: "Ah' so ben io che sta'l mio sol qui dentro." We also hear again that he is returning, coming back to a place where he has spent time before, "E pur io torno qui."

This is followed by a ritornello, another passage of song, another ritornello, another song, and so on: four ritornellos altogether and four sung stanzas. This leads to more questions and more speculation that will be answered in the singer's preparation and in the rehearsal period. We know where Otto is coming from and where he is going. So why does he not go there directly? Why does he stop four times? Is he so excited that he has to stop and catch his breath? Is he having trouble believing he is almost there? Is he afraid that in his absence she might have changed? He says, "Apri un balcon, Poppea, col bel viso in cui son le sorti mie" (Open your window, Poppea, and show me that sweet face on which ever depends my fate), almost as if he wants some kind of reassurance. Does he stop often because his excitement is high, and he wants to relish it? That would puzzle him and make him hesitate. What we do not want to think, in the audience, is: oh, the director told him to sing a stanza, move to the next column, and sing again. If that is all the singer gives us to think about, then we might as well stay home and put on the CD.

Perhaps it is a mixture of all of these, or of some of them at different moments. The libretto is rich in images of seeing and clarification: Otto invites Poppea to "Sorgi, e disgombra omai da questo ciel caligini" (Wake, and disperse forever from our clear sky all murkiness). So perhaps what is slowing him down is his imagination, his capacity for seeing things in his mind. There is a rich array of choices. But each must be actable: for each choice, actions will have to be found so that we in the audience understand clearly what Otto is thinking. None of these actions is enough to change Otto's objective; in fact, their effect should be to intensify the strength of his desire. If this happens, if we in the audience can see Otto's desire intensifying, our own interest will be roused; the stakes for all of us will be higher.

Then, suddenly, there is a change. Otto sees something move in the darkness. He realizes that what he sees is not shadows or ghosts, but real men, soldiers: "Ma . . . ," he says (But . . .). He is making a *discovery*: if they are soldiers, they can only be Nero's guards.

Ma che veggio, infelice?	But—who lies here in the darkness?
Non già fantasmi o pur	These are not phantoms, these are no
notturne larve,	ghostly shadows—
Son questi i servi di Nerone.	They surely are posted here by Nero.

Here is the answer to the fourth question: *What stops him from getting what he wants?* and obviously this discovery will make Otto change. His objective will still be to get to Poppea, but now instead of simply walking into the house he has to deal with a new reality. So his intention—what he wants at this particular moment—cannot stay the same. He has to stay hidden and figure out why the guards are there. It is not hard to understand. He realizes he has been duped: Poppea and Nero are lovers. This is his second discovery.

. . . ahi dunque	. . . Ah heavens,
Agl'insensati venti	I have poured out my soul
Io diffondo i lamenti.	To the winds that cannot hear me,
Necessito le pietre	I must beg the senseless stones to
a deplorarmi,	show me pity.
Adoro questi marmi,	I worship blocks of marble,
Amoreggi con lagrime	I make love to this window with
un balcone,	my weeping,
E in grembo di Poppea	While on the breast of Poppea
dorme Nerone.	Nero lies sleeping.

At "ahi" the dynamic marking is *forte* with a crescendo following, as if to suggest that his response to this bursts out of him. His attitude changes. He can be angry, hurt, incredulous, sarcastic—the range of possibilities is broad, depending on the overall point of view of the director and the sensibility of the singer playing the role. Whatever his choice, Otto is finding that his world has changed dramatically. And Love's claim in the prologue—"dirà che'l mondo a' cenni miei si muta" (at Love's signal, the world is changed completely)—is turning out to be true. The culmination of what he discovers is another change. The old objective, wanting to be with Poppea, is blocked but not eliminated; his new intention is to hide himself and listen to the guards to see what more he can find out.

Once a response is chosen, it will affect the response to the next line and the next action; this choice will in turn affect the next, and so on. In this way the scene will be developed in a specific and dynamic way, step by step, moment by moment. And each moment produces a different response or feeling. Rehearsals are the time for experimenting with these choices, for seeing what works and what does not, for thinking up new choices. Nothing can be vague or left to chance. The music and the words provide the cues. Otto must be able to build from self-mockery ("agl'insensati venti io diffondo i lamenti" [I have poured out my soul to the winds that cannot hear me]) to anger ("Ah' perfida Poppea" [Ah, treacherous Poppea]), to hurt ("son queste le promesse e i giuramenti?" [is this the way you keep the promise I was given?]), and finally to a sense of helplessness ("ma l'aria e'l cielo a'damni miei rivolto" [now, raging, the elements have turned against me]).

To summarize: Otto returns; his objective is to be with Poppea. He discovers guards outside her palace. He realizes that they are Nero's guards and that this means Nero is with Poppea, is in fact her lover. Then the scene changes, the guards awaken, and Otto steps away, though he may stay onstage. He has a new intention: to hide so that he can learn what the guards have to say. Finding this new intention is his answer to the fifth question: *How does he get around the block?*

Act II, Scenes 11 and 12—Otto Confronts Poppea

The next time we see Otto, nine scenes later, much has happened. In Act I, scene 1, when he was listening to the guards, he had heard them talking about Nero's self-absorption: they said that so long as he got what he wanted he did not care about anyone else—his wife's suffering, revolts in the empire, nothing. We have seen Seneca, the philosopher, ineffectually counseling both Octavia and Nero; he has tried to argue that the emperor's desire for Poppea "non è colpa da rege o semideo: è un misfatto plebeo" (is unworthy of a ruler, a demi-godhead: it is a sin for a peasant); we have seen Nero's tantrum in response. So much for Virtue's claims in the prologue. The power of Love, by contrast, seems everywhere rampant, fueled by ambition.

When we see Otto this time, he is hiding once again. (This seems to be a frequent posture for him, lurking outside while the real action goes on elsewhere. Is it meant to be comic? Ironic? The way it is to be played is a decision for the director and singer to make in rehearsal.) Where is he coming from? Again, as for his first appearance (Act I, scene 1), neither text nor music offers information about where he may have been. Where he is coming from emotionally, though, is quite clear. Like any betrayed lover, he has been through the full range of feelings: humiliation, anger, despair, desire for revenge, desire to win his love back. So where he is coming from is from a state of turmoil. Where is he going? To confront Poppea. What does he want? To win her back, to punish her, to get revenge? We do not know, and the reason we don't know is that at the very moment he appears, he finds himself blocked again by Nero's presence. And that answers the question: what prevents him? Just as he did in his first scene, he must instantly change his intention, which answers the final question: how does he get around what is preventing him? Once again he is forced to hide.

From his hiding place, he overhears an ardent dialogue between the emperor and Poppea. This must be painful, hearing her say to her new lover what she might before have said to him. But he also learns something: just how ruthless Poppea is. He hears her telling Nero that Seneca is boasting "ch'il tuo scettro dipende sol da lui" (that your sceptre depends on his approval). In response, he hears Nero promise that Seneca will be dealt with and that "oggi vedrai quel che sa far Amore" (today you shall see Love victorious), meaning that Poppea will become empress. Otto realizes that Poppea is condemning Seneca to death; this is what she is capable of. He also sees that at this point she seems to have got everything she wants. All this must affect how he approaches Poppea when he finally has the chance.

The ritornello that introduces Otto's confrontation of Poppea has a military-sounding beat, suggesting conflict, but it is muted. This sets the terms for their meeting. It is the first time they have seen each other since he went away, when they were still lovers. From what he has just heard, we know where he is coming from: he has learned that her relationship with Nero is based almost entirely on ambition and sex. What is his objective— to win her back? Surprisingly, given what he has just heard, it seems to be. He begins regretfully:

Ad altri tocca in sorte	While others may drink deeply
Bere il licor, e me guardar il vaso,	Of the sweet wine, I only see the vessel.
Aperte stan le porte	If Nero comes, the door stands open wide.
A Neron, ed Otton fuori è rimaso;	Meanwhile Otto stands outside it.
Siede egli a mensa a satollar sue brame,	Nero at table enjoys the best of eating,
In amaro digiun mor'io di fame.	While in rigorous fast, Otto is dying.

To contrast himself the way he does with the man who now has what he wants is a little odd. These are not the words of a man crazed with suffering, or of an accuser; there is irony, but it is muted. What he seems to want to do is to show Poppea something, a picture of himself as noble sufferer. This, he hopes, will move her enough to change her objective and take him back. (The naivety of this might make Otto appear hopelessly out of his depth, if that is how the director and singer choose to play the scene; but it is not the only way the scene can be played.)

What is Poppea's objective? Clearly she does not want to be here. But a negative cannot be played; she cannot play "not wanting to be here." She has to find the positive to play; only this will give her the basis for her actions in the scene. *Where is she coming from?* From a meeting with her lover, the emperor, in which she has gotten everything she wants. *Where is she going?* To prepare to be empress. *What does she want?* She wants Otto to leave. *What prevents her* is that Otto is physically there and shows no sign of leaving. *How does she get around this obstacle?* She does several things.

When she speaks, she seems to meet Otto on his level: slightly detached, regretful. But she does not disguise her firmness, nor in fact her contempt.

Chi nasce sfortunato	Some men are born unlucky;
Di se stesso si dolga, e non d'altrui;	Their complaint should be made to themselves, not others.
Del tuo penoso stato	Although your state's unhappy,
Aspra cagion, Otton, non son nè fui:	I'm not the cause, Otto; I cannot help it.
Il destin getta i dadi e i punti attende:	It is Fate throws the dice and awaits the ending;
L'evento, o buono o reo, da lui dipende.	Events for good or evil are in Fate's keeping.

It is not she who is responsible for his suffering; it is not she who has betrayed him. It is Fate, who sets the rules at birth. Since he was born unlucky, he is only getting what Fate has handed him; it is not her fault. Her first way of getting around the obstacle that Otto represents, then, is to dismiss him by matching his tone but changing the terms of his argument.

It is obvious that what prevents Otto from achieving his objective is Poppea herself, and that his first tactic for overcoming this obstacle—showing her how he has suffered for her—has not worked. So he changes his intention: instead of trying to show her himself to get her to change, he holds a mirror up, to show her herself. But his objective—winning her back—evidently does not change.

Sperai che quel macigno,	Your heart, though hard and stony,
Bella Poppea, che fi circonda il core,	Lovely Poppea, I hoped might feel some pity,
Fosse d'amor benigno	Might be by Love's touch melted,
Intenerito a pro del	Seeing the proof of my pain and my

mio dolore,	great misery.
Or del tuo bianco sen la selce dura	But that hard flint you keep within your bosom
Di mie morte speranze. è sepoltura	Is the tomb where, unpitied, my hopes lie buried.

This too fails, and it forces Poppea to be more blunt. She knows that she has played with him, that he has suffered, and that he is angry. So, to try to bring the scene to an end, she makes it clear what she has probably always been interested in:

Deh, non più rinfacciarmi,	No more of these reproaches.
Porta, deh porta il martellino in pace,	You must endure your martyrdom in silence,
Cessa di più tentarmi	And no longer attempt to persuade me.
Al cenno imperial Poppea soggiace;	To imperial decree Poppea owes submission.
Ammorza il foco omai, tempra gli sdegni;	Stifle your sorrow, and quench fires of anger.
Io lascio te per arrivar ai regni.	By leaving you I hope to gain an Empire!

The sixteenth notes on the word "arrivar" (to arrive, to amount to) and the length of time she holds "regni" show pretty clearly what she really wants. Otto presses her by asking three times: "È questo del mio amor il guiderdone?" (And this is the reward of my devotion?). Poppea has some choices here. She may have a twinge of conscience. Or she may leave because she knows that if she stays longer she will call the guards—which is to say that she will destroy Otto, since that would be the consequence if Nero discovered that Otto had been her lover. But that is risky: it might also destroy her, since Nero would then find out about her affair with Otto. So the stakes in the scene are extremely high. Whatever her choice, on the line "Non più, son di Nerone" (No more. I turn to Nero), she exits.

There's a fermata. Silence. And tension—what is Otto to do now? The encounter has been brief and, on Poppea's part, direct. All his subtle efforts with her have failed, and she has very unsubtly shown him what she is. Otto now has to take stock. He needs to make a transition: he must recover from the shock of what he has learned (this is where he is coming from), and he must decide what to do (this is where he is going). He must find a new objective. When he is ready to move on, there's a quiet chord. The music of this scene is not violent; it is marked *legato*. This says something about Otto's actions during the transition, but what? Is he controlling himself? As he takes stock, he comments on the nature of women: "il più imperfetto sesso non ha per sua natura altro d'uman in sé che la figura" (the weaker sex has nothing in its nature of true humanity save outward beauty). He realizes that Poppea is quite capable, once she has become empress, of having him killed. In effect, he is now a fugitive. What he wants, then, is to find some way of saving his life. That is his objective. The last lines of the scene show how difficult a transition this is for him:

<table>
<tr><td>A questo, a questo fine
  Dunque arrivar dovea
L'amor tuo, perfidissima Poppea!</td><td>To such a pass you've brought me,
I who have faithfully loved you,
O treacherous, treacherous Poppea!</td></tr>
</table>

How will he get around this? The answer is in the next scene. Drusilla, an attendant of Octavia, appears. She claims that she has always loved Otto, and she has come here to declare this and make him a proposition. So Otto will have another transition to make and a fresh objective to find.

In the meantime, the gods of the prologue, watching from their airy home, will have further occasion to ponder their debate and be amused by the vexed lives of the mortals below.

Action in Verdi's *La traviata*, Act I

Though there is always action in an opera, not all actions are the same.

Action can be internal as well as external. For example, action occurs within a character's mind whenever thought occurs. Since thought occurs all the time, any movement a character chooses to make is simply the externalization of an idea that has already been thought. It is always interesting to see a singer think, to see his or her thought revealed in the action that follows the thought.

Action must not be thought of as movement. Movement cannot be a substitute for thought. Bernard Shaw, who wrote speeches for his characters that sometimes covered three or four pages, demanded that his actors slow down the delivery of a speech. The faster the speech is spoken, the less chance we have of following the argument being presented, and thus, paradoxically, the longer the speech seems. The same is true of physical movement. The more a character moves without thought, simply for the sake of trying to be interesting or to fill the time, the longer the aria or scene will feel. Stillness allows us to see the character at work. As Figaro is developing his ideas for revenge on the Count in "Se vuol ballare," we need to see him think, not move, through his ideas.

One of the great onstage thinkers in English drama is Hamlet. It is he who, when he meets the traveling players whom he is going to use in his plot to catch his father's killer, brashly gives them instructions about their art:

Nor do not saw the air too much with your hand thus, but use all gently; for in the very torrent, tempest, and as I may say, whirlwind of passion, you must acquire and beget a temperance that may give it smoothness. . . . Be not too tame neither, but let your own discretion be your tutor. Suit the action to the word, the word to the action. (*Hamlet,* Act III, scene 2)

Hamlet himself is the model of this "discretion." Each of his soliloquies is dense with thought, with fears and desires probed and rejected, conflicts explored, discoveries made. How distracting it would be to an audience if, in the soliloquy "To be or not to be," an actor were to pace back and forth, sawing the air with his hands, as if walking out the ideas of his internal debate. The power of the soliloquy is there, in the language, and it is intensified if the actor is able to be still and to show in this stillness the power of his great question: should I live or die?

The aria is the singer's equivalent of the actor's soliloquy. It is in the aria that thoughts occur most intensely and most revealingly. Hamlet's advice is sound. It is the words with the music that reveal these thoughts and give clues to the action needed.

Often, in musical passages when a character is not singing or there is a fermata over a silence, a singer or director feels that some physical movement must be made so the audience will not be bored by either the silence or the stillness. In fact, though, the very opposite is true. To see a character thinking and then see the results of those thoughts in the next beat commands us to watch. Movement is the result of the thought. Stillness can command our attention.

Violetta ends the first act of Verdi's *La traviata* with a particularly strong and revealing recitative and aria. For most of both she is absorbed by her thoughts, debating within herself the question that Verdi has forced on her. For the singer, deciding what to do is a challenge. She is alone on the stage for about twelve minutes, and she has very difficult music to sing, difficult not just because it is hard to sing but because it is so demanding dramatically. Perhaps there are words and music that seem to require movement; perhaps at other times stillness is more appropriate—how to know? The solution lies first in coming to understand the role of the aria in the act as a whole and then working through the aria and its recitative, following the structure of its thoughts and feelings and learning what the acting choices are.

The whole action of *La traviata* is remarkably economical, focused, and powerful. It begins in an opulent setting, full of beautifully dressed guests being welcomed by Violetta; it ends in a garret where Violetta is dying, poor and almost alone. It begins with Violetta as a successful courtesan, unexpectedly wooed by Alfredo (a young man from outside her normal world who has fallen in love with her); it ends with a reconciliation between these two lovers—a reunion that comes too late to save her. In between are mistakes and misunderstandings, acts of great foolishness and great nobility.

The opera opens at a fashionable ball being given by Violetta. She has been ill; the ball is her signal that she is better—or that she wants to be better. To the celebration comes a shy young man, Alfredo. We learn that he has secretly admired Violetta; this is his chance to be introduced to her. A friend provokes him into toasting Violetta; she replies; the guests go into another room to dance; Alfredo finds an opportunity to declare his love; Violetta puts him off, but, strangely (to her as well as to him), invites him to visit her next day; he leaves in ecstasy; she is left alone to think about what has happened and what she has done. In fact, by the end of Act I—as a result of the aria we will look at—Violetta finds she can return Alfredo's love. As Act II begins, we discover that they have moved to a house in the country; they need money, so Violetta sells off some possessions; Alfredo finds out about this, is ashamed of himself, and leaves to get money in Paris; Alfredo's father appears and begs Violetta to give him up for the sake of his unmarried younger daughter, whose prospects will be damaged by Alfredo's liaison with a courtesan; she protests at first, then agrees and writes to Alfredo that she is leaving him and going back to Paris, to her former protector, the Baron, but does not tell him about his father's visit. Alfredo returns, discovers the letter, and is enraged; he thinks she has simply grown tired of him and gone back to her old life. He follows her to Paris; at a party where she appears with the Baron, he insults her and challenges the Baron to a duel. Later, alone and dying, Violetta hears that Alfredo has finally learned about her sacrifice and is coming to ask her forgiveness; he appears and they are reconciled; forgetting her condition, they plan a new life together; his father comes in and begs Violetta to forgive him; Violetta feels her strength return, but it is only for a moment, and she dies.

In the first act, the point toward which all the action moves is Violetta's aria at the end and the discoveries she makes there. Preparation for it therefore starts at the beginning of the act, so that when Violetta gets to the aria she is clear about where she is coming from and what she wants—so that she knows why she has to sing what she is singing.

The first act of *La traviata* takes place in a single setting. The action moves rapidly but always coherently from the most public kind of social encounter, a party, to the most private, a young man's declaration of love and a woman's thoughts about what she has heard. In the space of a single act,

Violetta has a great distance to travel. At the beginning, she is the hostess of the party and the focus of everyone's attention; then she is the recipient of Alfredo's ardent declaration; finally she is left alone to think. As we watch her progress, we can see that there are stages and changes: she has a certain objective at the beginning of the act; she makes discoveries that force her to change this objective; at every stage she faces significant obstacles to getting what she wants; and the discoveries she makes deeply affect her and lead her to further change. We can also see one of the qualities at work that makes these changes possible: Violetta is a very good listener. She pays attention to what is being said to her and who the speaker is. The changes she makes over the course of the act—and the opera—do not make any sense unless the audience can perceive her ability to listen.

In the audience we do not learn right away where Violetta is coming from,[1] but the singer playing Violetta knows it from her first read-through: Violetta is coming from an illness that is serious enough for her to have been confined to her room. Later in the act we see her struggling with faintness. Questions arise. Does Violetta know how ill she is? Should she act right from the beginning as if she were an invalid? As if she were ill but defying her illness? Should she show any signs of illness at all? If she is so ill, why is she giving this party? I have seen productions of both *Bohème* and *Traviata* where it was clear from each singer's first entrance that she knew she was going to die. This, as you can imagine, gave the productions a lugubrious tone. But both operas are about life and love. To play the end of the opera at the beginning drains the characters of their energy and joy. Weeping willows are great in gardens but not on the stage. No one should enter any scene knowing the end of it.

The party has already begun, and guests are arriving; she is going to greet them. Violetta tells us quickly what she wants. Two friends ask her if she's able to enjoy the party she's giving. She wants to enjoy herself, she says:

Lo voglio;	I want to;
Al piacere m'affido, ed	I entrust myself to pleasure, and
io soglio	with that drug
Con tal farmaco i mali sopir.	I dull my sufferings.

What prevents her from enjoying herself is her illness, her "sufferings." She is trying to overcome this, to the extent that she can, by giving a party and trying to have fun. Pleasure is her drug—but not a drug meant to cure.

---

1. From this point on I don't mention the five questions specifically, though my comments assume that they are being asked.

Rather, it is intended to suppress her symptoms, like a narcotic; it is what she takes so she will not feel how ill she is. Why is she so determined to have fun? Is she giving the party just to show she can, to defy her illness? Is she trying to reassure her protector, the Baron, since she knows no one wants a mistress who is ill? Or is she keeping busy so she can avoid thinking about her life? Whatever answers are chosen, Violetta cannot be played as an invalid, waiting for her next cough. For her the stakes are, from the beginning, high. So it seems that her objective as the scene begins is to defy her illness by finding pleasure where she can.

That is the set-up. That is who Violetta is when we first see her welcoming her guests. Then a new person is introduced, Alfredo. He is presented as "un altro che molto v'onora" (another who esteems you greatly). It quickly becomes clear that, with Alfredo, some kind of new value is being introduced as well: Gastone, who presents him, says quietly to Violetta that Alfredo thinks of her constantly; when she was ill "ogni dì con affanno qui volò, di voi chiese" (every day he rushed here anxiously, and asked about you). To that, she says: "Cessate, nulla son io per lui" (Stop; I am nothing to him). But just how does she say this? Is she annoyed? Suspicious? Amused? Whatever answer the actor chooses, she must then ask, why? Once a choice is made, the next few actions will be determined by that choice. Gastone says, "Non v'inganno" (I'm not deceiving you). This suggests that Violetta, in the line above, may be both suspicious and a little amused. She says, "Vero è dunque? ... onde è ciò? ... nol comprendo" (Is it true then? ... Why is this? ... I don't understand). Why would she be suspicious? One reason might be that she has never met a man who does not want something from her, usually sex. Alfredo, who has been listening intently to all of this, says with a sigh, "Sì, egli è ver" (Yes, it is true).

What is new here is values that Violetta might not have expected: a kind of earnestness, even sincerity. Since they are new, she will have to react to them. She turns quickly to the Baron, her protector: "Voi, Barone, non feste altrettanto" (You, Baron, didn't do as much). Why does she attack the Baron? Does she want Alfredo to know she belongs to the Baron? Does she want to embarrass him? Is she embarrassed by Alfredo's attention and eager to hide it? Is she surprised, perhaps a little moved, by what he seems to represent, and does she therefore need a distraction to help her deal with it? She is pretty sure that these are not values the Baron shares: "Vi conosco da un anno soltanto," he says (I've known you only for a year); to which she quickly replies, "Ed ei solo da qualche minuto" (And he only for a few minutes).

So Violetta has learned some things: that a young man is present who is interested in her in a different way than most of the men who are at this party would be, including the Baron. What does she do with these discoveries? Does her objective—to enjoy herself as much as she can—change? No. What does change, though, is that she has a new intention: to draw Alfredo out, to find out more about him and about what he has to say.

Just at this moment, however, Alfredo is silent. Why? Is he shy? Is he surprised by what he has just heard himself say? Does he need a moment to pull himself together? His friends are good at banter—perhaps this would make him more silent; perhaps it could provoke him. Gastone tries to do just this: "E tu dunque non apri più bocca?" (Aren't you going to open your mouth any more?). The Marquis says to Violetta, "È a madama che scuoterlo tocca" (It's up to Madame to stir him). So she does: she knows how to charm (it is how she makes her living); she says, "Sarò l'Ebe che versa" (I'll be Hebe and pour"). To her he can respond, and quickly he picks up the allusion: "E ch'io bramo immortal come quella" (And I hope as immortal as she). (Hebe was the daughter of Zeus and Hera, the personification of youth and beauty, the cup-bearer of the gods, and the wife Hercules was given when he was taken up to Olympus. Few of us will get this; perhaps not many got it in Verdi's day. But that is not the point. The point is that understanding it can help both singers as they prepare their roles.) There is humor here, and one of the tasks of a singer in creating a role is to find the humor in the text for the particular character. There are many kinds of humor—ironic, vicious, raucous, self-deprecating, and so on—and it is to be found everywhere, including in the highest of tragedies. Violetta can make her allusion to Hebe playfully, suggesting perhaps that his attentiveness might be heroic; if she is a Hebe, he might be a Hercules. Alfredo's reply is a chivalrous expression of hope that she will get over her illness. Most important, what all this seems to show is that even at this stage they have established a special rapport. They are both well read enough to make and pick up classical allusions, and they are both paying enough attention to each other to converse in what is almost a private language, all at the level of witty banter. Gastone presses for a toast. First he asks the Baron; the Baron shakes his head. (Question for the Baron: why does he refuse?) So Gastone turns to Alfredo, inviting him to do the honors. But Alfredo says no: "L'estro non m'arride" (Inspiration isn't favoring me). Gastone asks whether he isn't a master of verbal invention, and Alfredo turns and says to Violetta, "Vi fia grato?" (Would you like it?). Her response is a monosyllable: "Sì" (Yes). Then a fermata. The music shows that the stakes are rising for Alfredo and that he has a decision to make: does he give the toast or doesn't he? Does he reveal himself further or not? He stands: "Sì? (another fermata, matching Violetta's), "... L'ho già in cor" (Yes? ... It's in my heart already). There are twenty bars of introduction ending in a fermata, and then his toast, the "Brindisi," begins.

Because the stakes here are high for him, we need to know more about Alfredo. Just what is his position at this point in the scene? How comfortable is he in this milieu? Does he know anything about it, apart from his friendship with Gastone? How naive is he? How innocent? Answering these questions will help the singer clarify where Alfredo is coming from. Evidently he has entered a society with which he is unfamiliar, although he is with a friend, Gastone, who knows it well. It is a society of rich men and kept women, and it is devoted to pleasure, defined strictly, it seems, as gambling, dancing, drinking, and love. Since the women are kept, not married, we can assume that the love undertaken here is primarily sexual, not romantic, at least not romantic in a sense that Alfredo, who called at Violetta's house every day to find out how she was, would understand. The people in this society are comfortable being at this party, and they are very attentive; at least the ones around Violetta are. They pay close attention to what is being said and who's saying it. Is Alfredo self-conscious? Would this attentiveness increase his self-consciousness? Is he a little nervous? He has an objective in coming to the party, however: to be introduced to Violetta, and to win her if he can. His objective allows him to sweep aside these obstacles. Standing up in this company to propose a toast is a bit like the action of a hero intent on winning his lady. For Alfredo it might seem to be a heroic—a Herculean—task.

Here is his toast, the Brindisi:

Libiamo, libiamo ne' lieti calici	Let us drink, drink from the happy goblets
Che la bellezza infiora;	That beauty embellishes;
E la fuggevol ora	And let the fleeting hour
S'innebri a voluttà.	Intoxicate itself with pleasure.
Libiam ne' dolci fremiti	Let us drink in the sweet trembling
Che suscita l'amore,	That love arouses,
(indicando Violetta)	*(pointing to Violetta)*
Poichè quell'occhio al core	Since that eye goes
Onnipotente va.	All-powerful to the heart.
Libiamo, amore, amor fra i calici	Let us drink, among the cups,
Più caldi baci avrà.	Love will have warmer kisses.

Alfredo begins by using the language of his setting, the party. He speaks of "la bellezza," of "la fuggevol ora," of the "dolci fremiti che suscita l'amore." Of course he is speaking of Violetta: she is the beauty, the pleasure he imagines is associated with her, and all that pleasure belongs to the fleeting hour. These are terms and images of hedonism, of *carpe diem*, of pleasure for its own sake. But then he changes. Deliberately he turns to her. Whereas just before he had spoken of "la bellezza," now the "occhio al core onnipotente va." Whereas before he spoke only of "voluttà," now he calls for the kind of love that "più caldi baci avrà." Clearly the kind of experience Alfredo is invoking with these images is not just hedonistic, it is deeper and fuller. We would call it love, and we would call his song a declaration to Violetta of his love.

Obviously she must reply, and she does.

Tra voi saprò dividere	Among you I will share
Il tempo mio giocondo;	My time of joy;
Tutto è follia nel mondo	All is folly in the world
Ciò che non è piacer.	That isn't pleasure.
Godiam, fugace e rapido	Let us enjoy ourselves, love's joy
È il gaudio dell'amore;	Is quick and fleeting;
È un fior che nasce e muore,	It's a flower that is born and dies,
Nè più si può goder . . .	Nor can it be enjoyed again . . .
Godiam . . . c'invita un fervido	Let us enjoy ourselves . . . feverish,
Accento lusinghier.	Enchanting words invite us.

Her reply takes the form of a counter-argument: she takes the terms that Alfredo has used and redefines them to suit herself. She denies that love is, as he said, "onnipotente." By contrast, her image of love is the opposite of "all-powerful": it is "un fior che nasce e muore." By choosing this metaphor, she is denying that love has anything to do with the heart; she is claiming that it can never last, that its life is as short as a flower's. What she seems to mean by love, then, is simply pleasure. The implication of "fervido" is that the aim of this pleasure is its intensity, not the person with whom it's being shared ("fervido" also reminds us of her illness, and of the kinds of activities she uses to mask it). So this is the answer she wants to give to Alfredo's declaration, to his invitation to "più caldi baci." His claim is for the powerful experiencing of the beginnings of love; her reply is for love's ephemerality.

Why does she feel she has to answer Alfredo back, almost to put him in his place? Well, his words must have had an effect on her: otherwise she would never waste the time. His words have made her think of things she may not very often think of, and this may be uncomfortable. For example, they have made her begin to confront the shallowness of the kind of love she practices. She is a courtesan, after all: to survive in this role means that she has to avoid intimacy that might develop into genuine love; she has to repress her feelings in order to make her living. His words may also force her to face the transitory nature of her profession—the impermanence of her lovers and, most emphatically, the ephemeral nature of her own existence. That would hardly be surprising, given that we know she is coming from her illness. Perhaps this helps us understand why she makes such a dramatic claim for pleasure. "Tutto è follia nel mondo ciò che non è piacer," she says. That is a pretty desolate vision: can she really believe that nothing in life is worth living for except pleasure, "fugace e rapido?" Evidently she can, whether she is fully aware of what she is saying or not.

From the beginning of the act, we know that Violetta's pursuit of pleasure is also a way of avoiding the reality of her illness. Now we can see that her pursuit of pleasure is also a way of avoiding or protecting herself from another reality: the knowledge of how empty her life is. How aware of this is she?

After the chorus has finished (they have four lines after Violetta's response to Alfredo), we see that she cannot let the subject drop: "La vita è nel tripudio" (Life is pleasure), she says again to Alfredo, insistently. "Quando non s'ami ancora" (When one isn't yet in love), he says, not letting her finish. She picks this up: "Nol dite a chi l'ignora" (Don't speak of it to one who doesn't know it). In fact, this *is* her truth—what she *does* know, thanks to his reminders, is that love is what she has never experienced. It also tells him what he needs to know in order to keep pursuing her: whatever the nature of her present life, she is still emotionally untouched and therefore still available. "È il mio destin così" (That is my destiny), he says. And with their mutual discoveries, the first part of Act I comes to a close.

What has Violetta discovered? She has heard something from Alfredo that has shaken her, words that force her to think about what pleasure— her way of being alive—really means. (Remember: although Alfredo has seen her from a distance, she has never seen him before this party.) Her objective at the beginning was just that: to show that she could have a good time, that she was alive. Then, as she was introduced to Alfredo and began to pay attention to what he had to say, she acquired the intention of trying to find out more. Next, what she heard in the Brindisi—his claim for the power of love, his directing that claim at her—forced her toward a fresh intention: to defy these claims and justify her own way of life. And finally, in their few lines of dialogue after the "Brindisi," she has heard herself admitting to a relative stranger something she has probably always known and yet always tried to avoid thinking about—that her life is empty: "Nol dite a chi l'ignora." This is an astonishing moment for Violetta. Yet if she had not already known it at some level, nothing Alfredo could have said would have got through her armor; it is that knowledge now entering into consciousness that she takes into the next part of the first act, to Alfredo's wooing of her, and finally to her recitative and aria at the act's end, "È strano."

■ ■ ■

At the beginning of the next scene, Violetta wants to go into the ballroom to dance with her guests. Instead, she almost faints. Why? Because she is ill and weak. Yet there may be other reasons as well. She may be faint from the exertion of engaging in the debate with Alfredo. She may feel faint from having realized how empty her life is. She may find the effort of continuing with her party too great. The fainting gives Alfredo the chance to woo her. But we have to remember that at the beginning of this scene Violetta's objective is the same as it was at the beginning of the opera: to show that she can still be lively and vivid, that she can enjoy herself.

Verdi brackets this pivotal scene between Alfredo and Violetta with the chorus: at the beginning they go into the next room to dance, and at the end, "riscaldati dalle danze" (flushed from their dancing), they come back to take their leave. In between, Alfredo woos Violetta to a degree that perhaps surprises her, and perhaps even himself. She listens to him. Alfredo begins with his concern over the state she is in and a wish that he could take care of her: "Oh! Se mia foste, custode veglierei pe' vostri soavi dì" (Oh! If you were mine, like a guardian, I'd watch over your peaceful days). The climax of his wooing is his great aria "Un dì felice" (One happy day), which contains his definition of love and his offering of it to her:

Di quell'amor, quell'amor ch'è palpito	In that love which is the pulse
Dell'universo, dell'universo intero,	Of the universe, the whole universe,
Misterioso, altero,	Mysterious, aloof,
Croce e delizia al cor.	The heart's cross and delight.

Before his aria, she was amazed that anyone could have these feelings for her: "Che dite? . . . ha forse alcuno cura di me?" (What are you saying? . . . Does anyone really care for me?). But after it, there is a change: it seems that she wants to believe him. She offers him a flower and invites him to bring it back when it has withered, "domani" (tomorrow). He leaves, ecstatic; they sing their "Addio" almost as if it were a love duet. Yet each iteration of "addio" is different: his anticipates tomorrow; hers wonders about it.

Each "addio" has a very specific meaning. The relationship of Alfredo and Violetta is enriched with this careful analysis. It is not generalized "love," it is a specific and focused scene in which we see a relationship developing that leads to genuine love.

At once Verdi brings the chorus in to say good-bye, which they do, quickly and noisily; this moment is a direct contrast with the intensely private scene Violetta has just shared with Alfredo. Then she is left alone. To do what? At the beginning of the scene, her objective was to join the dancers. That was blocked by her fainting attack. And that allowed Alfredo to speak of what was in his heart. The dramatic contrasts in the scene—her fainting, Alfredo's declaration, his aria, their farewell duet, and the chorus's noisy entrance and exit—signal the magnitude of the contrasts that now exist for her. What is her objective now, at the end of the scene, after all that has happened? She is alone at last.

To do what? Her party is over, and the guests have left. Not one of them thought to ask how she was. Around her lies only the debris of pleasure. She met a man who said he loves her and wants to take care of her. She responded to him by giving him a flower and inviting him to come back the next day. She is going to bed—significantly, alone; no Baron. To understand what she wants, we should bear in mind all she has been through: the exertion of giving a party while trying to conceal her illness, and now this new emotional call on her strength. What she likely wants is rest, ease. But there is a block: her mind is full. She is agitated and cannot rest. She needs to deal with the events of the evening. So she ranges in her mind over them, thinking things through, reasoning, clarifying, trying to understand what has happened. What Alfredo is, and especially what he seems to offer, challenge the whole way she lives her life. Her objective now is to sort all this out so that she can get some rest.

The recitative that introduces the aria is made up of a series of rapid, intensely felt discoveries. Each discovery is a separate, complete thought in itself, and each conditions what follows: action, acting choices, and new discoveries. All the discoveries, in sequence, lead directly into the aria.

The recitative begins with silence: there is no accompaniment in the orchestra for three bars and no tempo marking, so the singer is free to decide when she wants to start singing. Because there is silence, the audience's attention falls entirely on Violetta. It is up to her to choose the action that will let her begin to sing. Does she take off her gloves? Does she collapse into a chair? Does she pour herself a glass of wine? Or does she just stand still? What triggers "È strano!" (It's strange!)—the sight of the chair Alfredo sat in? The memory of him standing by a table, or moving closer to take the flower from her? Or her own discoveries about herself?

È strano! ... è strano! ...
    in core
	It's strange! ... it's strange! ...
	    those words

Scolpiti ho quegli accenti!	Are carved in my heart!

Saria per me sventura un serio
    amore?
	Would a serious love be a misfortune
	    for me?

Che risolvi, o turbata
    anima mia?
	What are you resolving, O
	    my anguished spirit?

Null'uomo ancora t'accendeva ...	No man ever aroused you before ...
Oh gioia ch'io non conobbi,	O joy I did not know,
Esser amata amando! ...	To be loved and to love! ...
E sdegnarla poss'io	And can I spurn it
per l'aride follie del viver mio?	For the barren follies of my life?

At once there are more questions. What does "È strano ... è strano ..." mean? What is strange? There's a fermata right after the second "è strano," as if to let her remember and, at once, into her mind comes what Alfredo said. So it is his words that are strange: "In core scolpito ho quegli accenti!" The music shows a crescendo as she realizes what she is saying. She has made her *first discovery*: how strong an impact Alfredo's words have had on her. This is a new experience for her, having a man's words affect her so. It is a discovery that we in the audience must make with Violetta. Does she welcome this revelation? Violetta has some choices: should she sing this with anger, resenting the power of his words, or with wonderment? Her choice will affect how she sings the lines that follow. The memory of his words almost takes her breath away. She knows what her life consists of and how dramatic a change his words offer. So, immediately comes the question: "Saria per me sventura un serio amore?" This must be the first time she has ever uttered this thought, and a thought once spoken cannot be taken back: it must be followed through. Verdi helps her to do this. As she asks the question, the orchestra is silent; then, when she is silent, the music of the question reappears, but in a different rhythm: there are three clusters of sixteenth notes, as if to suggest a heartbeat. She is beginning to think about her own heart, about what a serious love would really mean. The music shifts to a minor key, perhaps ominously, foreshadowing a danger. (Although it does not stay there for long; it switches back and forth between the major and the minor keys—perhaps simulating her unrest?) Could love be dangerous to her? How so? As if provoked by this, she asks another question: "Che risolvi, o turbata anima mia?" She takes stock, examines what she feels, and puts it into the context of her past. There is another sixteenth-note cluster, this time more muted. It takes her back into her heart again and leads her to her *second discovery*, her understanding of why she is so moved by Alfredo's words: "Null'uomo ancora t'accendeva . . . Oh gioia ch'io non conobbi, esser amata amando!" The revelation astonishes her. Is this naive? No. When you do not have something, you do not know you miss it. She has never had this kind of attention before, and it awes her—or frightens her, or shocks her. This is her *third discovery*: the realization that the "gioia" is mutual. And this, in turn, leads to the question, "E sdegnarla poss'io per l'arida follie del viver mio?" She is at last fully aware of the emptiness of the life she is leading, at last able to admit it to herself. And this is her *fourth discovery*, the climax of the series. The alternatives are now clear. She has come to a point where she can no longer speak, she has to sing; the recitative is over, the aria begins. Her objective is still the same: to find a way of resolving her turmoil so that she can get some rest.

Verdi helps her make the transition from recitative to aria. There's a fermata, the key shifts to F minor, and a new tempo, marked *andantino*, is established. There are four bars in which she is quiet: three ascending triplets in the woodwinds marked *leggero*, then a pulsating rhythm (suggesting the deliberateness of her thinking?) marked *pianissimo*. And then she begins.

Ah fors'è lui che l'anima	Ah, perhaps he is the one whom my spirit,
Solinga ne' tumulti	Alone amid tumults,
Godea sovente pingere	Often enjoyed painting
De' suoi colori occulti . . .	With its mysterious colours . . .
Lui, che modesto e vigile	He who, modest and constant,
All'egre soglie ascese,	Came to my sickroom door,
E nuova febbre accese	And kindled a new fever
Destandomi all'amor.	Waking me to love.
A quell'amor, quell'amor ch'è palpito	To that love which is the pulse
Dell'universo, dell'universo intero,	Of the universe, the whole universe,
Misterioso, altero,	Mysterious, aloof,
Croce e delizia al cor.	The heart's cross and delight.
A me, fanciulla, un candido	When I was a girl, an innocent
E trepido desire	And timid desire
Quest'effigiò dolcissimo	Depicted him, the tender
Signor dell'avvenire,	Lord of my future,
Quando ne' cieli il raggio	When I saw in the skies
Di sua beltà vedea,	The glow of his beauty,
E tutta me pascea	And I fed myself wholly
Di quel divino error.	On that divine fancy.
Sentia che l'amore è palpito	I felt that love is the pulse
Dell'universo intero,	Of the whole universe,
Misterioso, altero,	Mysterious, aloof,
Croce e delizia al cor.	The heart's cross and delight.

(Resta concentrata un istante, poi, si scuote.)	*(She is lost in thought for a moment then she recovers herself.)*
Follie! . . . follie! . . .	Folly! . . . Folly! . . .
delirio vano è questo! . . .	This is vain raving! . . .
Povera donna, sola,	A poor woman, alone,
Abbandonata in questo	Abandoned in this
Popoloso deserto	Crowded desert
Che appellano Parigi,	That they call Paris,
Che spero or più? . . .	What more can I hope for now? . . .
Che far degg'io . . . Gioire!	What must I do? . . . Enjoy myself!
Di voluttà ne'vortici perir!	Perish in the giddy whirl of pleasure!
Gioir! . . . Gioir! . . .	Enjoy myself! . . . Enjoy! . . .
Sempre libera degg'io	Always free I must
Folleggiare di gioia in gioia,	Dart lightheadedly from joy to joy,
Vo' che scorra il viver mio	I want my life to glide
Pei sentieri del piacer.	Along the paths of pleasure.
Nasca il giorno, o il giorno muoia,	Whether the day is born or dying,
Sempre lieta ne' ritrovi,	Always gay at parties
A diletti sempre nuovi	My thought must fly
Dee volare il mio pensier.	Always to new delights.

The recitative was constructed out of a series of linked discoveries, the climax of which was her recognition of her life's barrenness, contrasted with the emotional fullness that Alfredo seemed to offer. The aria consists of two intensely imagined dramatic scenes. She thinks first of a kind of dream figure that used to come into her mind when she was ill, wondering if he was not some shadowy anticipation of the Alfredo who used to come by, before they had met, to ask after her. She then thinks back to her youth, and to how her "candido e trepido desire" created an ideal image of her love of the future. In each case the imaginary figure leads her to think of Alfredo; in each case she connects him with tenderness, concern, modesty, constancy—all values that are contrary to those of the world she lives in now. In each case the imaginary figures that lead her to Alfredo lead her also to Alfredo's great images of love, the love that is the "palpito dell'universo." So each imagined scene has its own climax and resolution as she repeats Alfredo's words, and at the end she seems to have fully committed herself to her new feelings. She seems to have achieved her objective, to have worked through her turmoil. And a new objective emerges: she now wants to have that love.

But a transition of three bars and a fermata leads in an unexpected direction, so we see that there is no resolution for her yet. "Follie!" she cries suddenly. After the dream comes the awakening. So there is a barrier to the new objective. She remembers who she is, and what she is: "Povera donna, sola, abbandonata." She feels despairingly the emptiness of her surroundings: "in questo popoloso deserto che appellano Parigi." She seems to have no means to counter this despair, no power to act, no hope: "Che far degg'io?," she asks, as if trying to decipher the inevitable. All she can do, she thinks, is what she knows how to do, what she has always done: "Gioire!" Her new objective, then, is to stay with pleasure, rejecting love. What is the barrier now? It is Alfredo and his love.

When Violetta cries out "Gioire!," what does she mean? Might she mean that she has no choice, that there is no escape for her from the crowded desert? So she has to choose pleasure because she thinks she has no other choice, she is trapped? Why would she be trapped? Or could "Gioire!" signal that she is choosing pleasure in order to avoid love—because she's afraid of love? Why? Because she thinks it would be madness for her to imagine she could be loved? Or that love could last? The choices the singer makes will affect her actions, including, for example, the way she sings "Gioire!"—with rage? despair? defiance? "Gioire!" occurs three times—or, more correctly, twice, with a final cadenza. Then, immediately: "di voluttà ne' vortici perir!" There is a fermata after "perir." Then, again, "Gioire!" is repeated, this time marked *dolce*, and the cadenza is marked *a piacere*, indicating that the tempo and structure of the cadenza are "at [the singer's] pleasure." Why *dolce*, especially when it follows so closely after "perir"? Could the second "gioire!" be full of passion and anger, the third of sorrow and regret? Then the cadenza: what could this suggest—determination, imposition of the will, desperation, rejection of the possibility of a new life? The cadenza seems to mark a transition, because at the end of it there is a fermata on the note as the orchestra moves into the introduction to "Sempre libera." This indicates that Violetta too is moving, making transitions from her state of mind at "Gioire!" (anger? despair? defiance?), through a rejection of the possibility that she could have a new life, and finally to some kind of acceptance of the life she has.

The introduction is eight bars long. So there are more choices to make. Does she maintain her defiance? Or does she look back briefly at her dream of love, looking at the vase of flowers (the famous camellias—the opera is based on the novel *La dame aux caméllias* by Alexandre Dumas *fils*), perhaps, then choose to move away, into her old life? At the end of the introduction there is another fermata. What is it for? Is she still holding back? From what? From letting go of her dream? Interestingly, "Sempre libera" begins *piano*. Does she again have a doubt? If so, it passes quickly once she enters fully into the aria. "Sempre libera" is driven by resolution and determination, though whether these feelings are born of defiance, despair, a genuine belief in what she is saying, or simply the desire to escape the pain of the new sensations of love is again something for the performer to decide. Regardless of her reasons, Violetta is relentless in her protestations, rejecting even the idea of love. But that relentlessness indicates that she thinks she has successfully achieved her objective: she has gotten over her obstacle—the turmoil caused by thoughts of Alfredo's love—and is now ready to go to bed. Once again Verdi sets up a transition: the completion of one thought, the movement to another.

And once again the transition leads to a reversal. She hears Alfredo's voice—in the street, in her head, it doesn't matter where. She realizes she is not at all free of her turmoil, that in fact nothing is resolved. What she hears is Alfredo at the climax of his appeal, his description of love as the "palpito dell'universo." And what that draws from her are yet more fervent repetitions of her desire to be free, whatever freedom may mean, expressed in more and more bravura singing. Her emotions twist and turn as her desperation increases. The music Verdi gives her, with its runs, cadenzas, melismas, leads her through these twists and turns. She hears Alfredo again. And suddenly, though she has no new words to sing, no new music, we know that she has changed. It is as if her thought is turning back upon itself. "Sempre libera" no longer means freedom from love, but the freedom to accept love. And the "gioia" she speaks of refers not at all to pleasure, but to love. So she turns, and leaves the room, truly and finally resolved. The aria has not ended the same way it began. She has achieved her objective and, whether she is going to her room to rest or to pack for a journey, we know that she is at peace.

I began this section asking how Violetta can decide when the words and music seem to require movement, and when stillness is more appropriate. Could the whole of her soliloquy be done without movement? In this recitative and aria, Violetta goes through tremendous, life-shaking discoveries; she makes choices that will profoundly affect her and others as well. Movement uses energy; if that energy is allied with her intention so that everything focuses on the one objective, then the ideas do not fight one another, and the energy is channeled: the movement—whatever it is— emerges naturally and clearly from the thought.

4

Playing Together

A RIAS GENERALLY PROVIDE opera's most vivid or arresting moments. Usually they are what we hum when we leave the theater. And yet, if singers act as well as sing, the scenes that prepare for the arias can be at least as dramatic (and will strengthen the effect of the arias themselves when they come). Scenes of conflict between characters, or groups of characters singing together but wanting different things, or even the same things, are what give energy to a production. Playing together is what gives operas' stories their legs.

Or not, as in a production of *Aida* I saw a while ago. The opera's final scene is intense. Radames, the hero, has been accused of betraying his country; he has been put alive into a tomb, sealed in to die. But his lament is not that he is going to die; rather, it is that he has lost the woman who has betrayed him but whom he also loves. He sees a shadow: "Una larva . . . una visione . . . No! forma umana è questa . . . Ciel! . . . Aida!" (A ghost . . . a vision . . . No! a human form . . . Heavens! . . . Aida!). She answers, "Son io" (It is I). It is a stunning moment of recognition, the climax of the entire opera. The two characters, who love each other with abandon, have finally come together. In the production I saw, though, neither singer so much as looked at the other. Not once! It seemed that each was so intent on singing impressively that any attempt at drama was abandoned for virtuoso display. There was not the slightest attempt even to pretend to act, no attempt to make the words mean anything, no playing together. The result? A concert, full of sound, empty of dramatic meaning.

Unless singers play with and to each other there can be no scene. And the comments I heard in the foyer after that *Aida* performance revealed the audience's puzzlement: "Why didn't they look at each other? I thought they were supposed to be in love." "They didn't even touch! Didn't they care?"

Playing together requires the ability to listen and hear and then respond to others, a clear understanding of what one's own character wants, and especially the ability to be precise and clear in action. We in the audience always need to believe that what we are watching is real; if there are two or three—or a crowd—onstage, we need to know very clearly who is doing what and why. Playing together also requires special qualities in performers—a willingness to submit their own particular wish to shine to the larger need of the piece. Rudolf Bing (for a long time the general director of New York's Metropolitan Opera) is reputed to have said, "We want an ensemble of stars, not comets." This is very much to the point: comets generally make their way through the sky alone; stars, however glittery each may be, shine together against the dark.

Here are two quite different kinds of scenes, from quite different composers, that show the power that can come from playing well together: the first from Verdi's *Falstaff*, written at the end of his career, and the second from Rossini's opera *L'italiana in Algeri*, written near the beginning of his. Each has different challenges for singers and directors alike. When these scenes done skillfully, they can be thrilling.

How to Play a Scene That Is a Lie: Verdi, *Falstaff*, Act II, Scene 1

Actions onstage can be external or internal. They can also be deliberately false.

In the theater, lying can be interesting to watch. Since we in the audience are safe from the consequences, it can be interesting indeed to watch liars practice their art. In the following, from Shakespeare's *Henry IV, Part 1*, Falstaff is lying through his teeth:

> *Falstaff*: I tell thee what, Hal, if I tell thee a lie, spit in
> my face, call me horse. (Act II, scene 2)

He is using two classic liar's tricks to help him: the claim that he is sincere, the dare to his listener to prove him wrong. Hal (the future King Henry V) knows what the truth of the particular situation is, and plays along, for the time being. There is an extra pleasure for an audience here: they know that Hal knows the truth, and they know that Falstaff does not know that Hal knows. So at this moment, the audience knows more than Falstaff does. They suspect that Falstaff is on his way to being caught, trapped in his lies, and they wait for this to happen, expecting unmaskings. They feel as if they are part of the plot.

When plots thicken, stirred by lies, singers have to be on their toes. Playing a lie is difficult. Singers are already playing roles: to play characters who are themselves playing roles is an extra challenge. And on top of that,

Mark Delavan as Falstaff in a 1999 New York City Opera production of Verdi's Falstaff.
(Photo by George Mott)

they have to make sure the audience knows what it needs to know: what is true and what is not.

Succeeding at lies requires close listening, watchfulness, and attention to the moment-by-moment building of a situation. Actions have to be chosen that will both convince victims and, at the same time, keep the audience clear about exactly what is going on. Detecting lies requires the same. Actions must be focused, and singers have to know precisely what their characters want in a scene, precisely with what (and whom) they are in conflict, and precisely how to manage all this, moment by moment, as the scene evolves. Although we have seen these skills deployed before in other scene studies, lying always raises the stakes and the potential consequences for the character. A scene of lies always raises the stakes for the audience as well.

One of the great lying scenes in opera takes place in the second act of Verdi's *Falstaff*, when Ford visits the old rascal. In this scene, though, it is not Falstaff who is the liar, but Ford, the husband of the woman Falstaff wants to seduce, the man whose money Falstaff plans to steal. Can Falstaff, the great master of deceit, see through the lies of another? Can Ford, not a liar by nature, avoid detection so that he can find out what he needs to know?

These questions are given particular point—and some poignancy—because of the way the opera's action unfolds. In fact, the entire opera is full of lies and deceptions. Each character is at some time involved in some kind of lie or disguise: in addition to the plotting of Ford and Falstaff, Alice and Meg Page concoct schemes to deceive, Bardolfo and Pistola mislead anyone they can almost by force of character, Mistress Quickly is both a schemer herself and the agent of schemers, Dr. Caius allows himself to be disguised, and even the young lovers, Nanetta and Fenton, though they are on the margins of the main plot, disguise themselves in the final scene so they can achieve their love. Lies, in this world, seem almost to be modes of survival. But if everyone is, to some extent, a liar, everyone is also, to some extent, the victim of a lie—except perhaps the young couple, who escape this only in the sense that they get exactly what they want.

It is Falstaff and Ford, though, who are the central figures. Both try to deceive others, and both are painfully deceived themselves. Both have to get beyond their lies and tactics so that they can rejoin the societies from which their deceits have exiled them: they have to accept that they have been wrong. Even Falstaff, who has never been part of any society for long, can at least get invited to dinner at the end.

All Falstaff's actions in the opera stem from two things: a truth and a lie. The truth is that he needs money: all he has in his purse, as Bardolfo finds out when he is told to look, is two marks and a penny. So he decides to go fortune hunting. The lie is one that he creates himself—and of which he becomes the victim. It all arises from what happened one day as he was out walking. He saw a vision:

Alice è il nome, e un giorno	Alice is her name; and one day
Come passar mi vide	As she saw me pass by
Ne' suoi paraggi, rise.	In her neighbourhood, she laughed.
M'ardea l'estro	Amatory fancy
Amatorio nel cor.	burned in my heart.
La Dea vibrava raggi	The Goddess cast rays
Di specchio ustorio.	Of a burning mirror.
(Pavoneggiandosi)	*(Swaggering)*
Su me, su me, sul fianco baldo,	On me, on me, on my bold flank,
Sul gran torace,	On my great chest,
Sul maschio piè, sul fusto saldo,	On my virile foot, on my solid trunk.
Erto, capace;	Erect, capacious;
E il suo desir in lei fulgea	And her desire shone in her
Sì al mio congiunto	So joined to mine
Che parea dir:	That she seemed to say:
"Io son di Sir John Falstaff."	"I am Sir John Falstaff's."

It is Alice's laugh, as she sees Falstaff, that sparks the lie: he fancies that she is laughing out of delight, out of desire for him. The truth and the lie come together in Falstaff's determination to seduce Alice and perhaps her friend Meg Page (the opera is based on both *Henry IV* and *The Merry Wives of Windsor*), winning both their love and access to their husbands' money boxes. But his self-deceit is pathetic, the pathos of an aging trickster who cannot protect himself from his own wishful thinking. There are other reasons Alice might have laughed as she saw Sir John, and they are not flattering to him.

Ford, by contrast, lies because of his obsessions—with his wife's fidelity, with the security of his cash, and with the chance he may appear ridiculous. His lies are tactics to protect himself and what he thinks of as his property. Like Falstaff, however, he is the victim of his obsession. It is true that Falstaff is plotting, but there is no real evidence that Ford's wife—or his money, or his reputation—are at risk. Ford believes they are because he is obsessed by the thought of losing them. So, like Falstaff, he believes a lie.

All scenes have facts and fictions. It is important that a singer, in his preparations—especially in an opera so replete with lies and deceptions as this one—comb through the scenes to find out what the basic, incontrovertible facts are. The synopsis that follows is a condensation of what singers playing

Falstaff and Ford could learn from their read-throughs of the entire opera, and from their breakdowns of the scenes they are in.

Falstaff

- He is down to his last penny. How do we know this? He tells Bardolfo to count the amount of money in his purse: Bardolfo finds two marks and a penny.
- He has a large appetite for food and wine. His love for anchovies, for example, is shown by the way Verdi sets the word "acciuga" on the whole note.
- His amatory appetites are as large, but they are not matched by a great self-awareness.
- He has an active and vivid imagination. He is capable of imagining things to be true simply because he wants them to be.
- He has written two letters, one to Alice Ford, one to Meg Page (in fact the letters are identical, which says something about Falstaff: that he does not waste his efforts—or perhaps that his imagination is limited). He plans to use these to seduce the women and gain access to their husbands' money.
- He wants Bardolfo and Pistola to deliver the letters.
- He has an artist's impatience with bad singing and bad stealing: he berates Bardolfo and Pistola for both.
- He cannot tolerate people who will not do his bidding: when Bardolfo and Pistola refuse to deliver his letters, he dismisses them with contempt.
- Alice and Meg have both received his letters, are outraged by them but also amused, and have decided to set a trap to punish him for his presumption.
- They both think he is ridiculous.

Ford

- He is told by Bardolfo and Pistola that Falstaff plans to seduce his wife and steal his money.
- Bardolfo and Pistola tell him that although they used to be in Falstaff's service, they have left him.
- Ford's wife, Alice, believes her husband to be very jealous: she says so to Meg.
- Ford is afraid of appearing ridiculous. We know that because he says it himself: he says he wants to "da me storno il ridicolo" (deflect ridicule from myself).

- He believes things because he wants to (like Falstaff). He wants to believe Bardolfo and Pistola, so he uses them in his plans to catch Falstaff in a trap. He tells them to announce him to Falstaff under a false name.
- Bardolfo and Pistola warn him that he needs to be extremely astute in dealing with Falstaff.

The second act opens with the execution of the plot of *The Merry Wives of Windsor*. Mistress Quickly is the messenger who must persuade Falstaff that Alice will be waiting for him. Because he is so sure of himself—and so vain—it is very easy for her to get him to take the bait. She leaves with the liaison arranged. At this point Ford is announced.

We need to understand something of the range of actions Falstaff and Ford can have in the scene between them, how the stakes are raised, and what basis they have for choosing their actions. First Falstaff. This is the high point of the opera for him. His dreams are about to be realized. Not only has he won the love of Alice (and Meg too, for all he knows), but he can also see his way clear to Ford's strongbox. He celebrates all this in his aria:

Alice è mia!	Alice is mine!
Va, vecchio John,	Go, old John,
Va, va per la tua via.	Go, go along your way.
Questa tua vecchia carne	This old flesh of yours
Ancora spreme	Still squeezes out
Qualche dolcezza a te.	Some sweetness for you.
Tutte le donne ammutinate	All women, in mutiny,
Insieme si dannano per me!	Damn themselves together for me.
Buon corpo di Sir John	Good body of Sir John,
Ch'io nutro e sazio,	That I nourish and sate,
Va, ti ringrazio.	Go, I thank you.

In a state of exultation, he is on his way to get ready for his tryst. His plan is to squeeze the most out of his encounter with Alice: not only her love, for an hour, but also, if he can, some of her husband's cash. To succeed, he has to dress for the occasion. What he wants at this moment is simply to get ready. But there is an interruption: Bardolfo and Pistola enter, to announce that there is a gentleman who wants to meet Falstaff—"un certo Mastro Fontana" (a certain Master Fountain)—and who has brought with him a demijohn of wine to help Falstaff break his fast. So his objective, to prepare to meet Alice, is interrupted. This does not remove the original objective, but it does replace it for the moment—with a temptation. This he deals with in his usual way: by giving into it. He invites Fontana to come in.

His intention, therefore, is to find out what the stranger wants and get the demijohn of wine.

The interruption creates a new *beat*. A beat—in the theatrical, *not* the musical, sense—is an action that is complete in itself. It is a way of breaking down a scene into playable moments and of clarifying the nature of the action. It can last for a page, ten pages, or a line. Falstaff's original objective was to get dressed for his "date." The effect of Ford's entrance is to make him suspend that objective temporarily. He has a new, short-lived (he hopes) intention. Each self-contained action that follows constitutes a beat. This term is useful because it allows players to identify significant small, fairly self-contained scenes that exist within larger scenes, and it can help them—working with the director in rehearsal—to create a rhythm in the way the scene's action develops and thereby give the whole scene dramatic shape.

We could say, for example, that Falstaff's aria of exultation, "Va, vecchio John," is itself a single beat. In dramatic terms it is all climax: it begins with Falstaff's cry "Alice è mia!" and modulates, without losing any of its mood of elation, into his song of gratitude to his body for carrying him along his way. It ends with Bardolfo's and Pistola's interruption, and this creates a transition to take the action into the next beat, Falstaff's first exchanges with Fontana. Other beats will take other dramatic shapes, as we shall see.

Fontana enters; it is Ford in disguise. He has learned that Falstaff is pursuing his wife—that he is perhaps about to be cuckolded. He has vowed (in Act I, scene 2) to find out the truth, to see exactly what Falstaff is up to and catch him in a trap. He has said to Bardolfo and Pistola, who had told him of Falstaff's plot:

A lui mi annuncierete,	You will announce me to him,
Ma con un falso nome,	But with a false name;
Poscia vedrete come	Then you will see how
Lo piglio nella rete.	I catch him in the net.
Ma . . . non una parola.	But . . . not a word.

He will be playing a role, then, assisted by Bardolfo and Pistola, who, for the moment, are on his side. We know from the read-through how Ford is affected by what they have told him. We see how strongly he reacts in his aria later in the scene and as he rampages through his own house looking for Falstaff in Act II, scene 2. So Ford is coming from a state of strong agitation. He is going to spring his trap, to find out exactly what Falstaff is up to and what his wife's role is. Of course, he could simply ask her, and that he does not raises questions. Why not? Is it because he wants to test her—to find out, without her knowing that he is worried (since that too would make him appear ridiculous), whether she is virtuous? Is it because he does not think she would tell him the truth? Would it be humiliating for him to ask? He can see what Falstaff looks like: might he wonder what his wife could see in such a man? If she could be wooed by such a man, what would that say about her—and about Ford himself? These questions all intensify his need to find out the truth. They also intensify his agitation and therefore add to his burden, the need to control himself. Three things could get in the way. First, since we know how agitated Ford is, he must keep his temper under control if he wants to trap Falstaff and discover the truth. So he will have to behave in a way that is the exact opposite of his natural inclination. Secondly, Bardolfo and Pistola are uncertain allies at the best of times; perhaps they are playing a game of their own. And thirdly, he may not be skillful enough to get Falstaff to tell him what he wants to know.

That is the set-up to the scene. Falstaff, who is confident that his own plot is succeeding—he has got Alice to agree to meet him—meets a man he does not know who offers him wine, which Falstaff is always happy to have. The interruption of his plans by this man is likely not particularly significant, he thinks, and may even be beneficial. So in this encounter he can be fairly relaxed. His intention (not his new objective) is to find out what this stranger wants so that he can get back to his preparations (his original objective), taking the wine with him if he can. However, since he has never met Fontana, he has to be careful: he has to make sure Fontana does not have an agenda of his own that might harm him, that Fontana is not setting some kind of trap for him. After all, why should a complete stranger be so generous? For Ford, on the other hand, the stakes are higher: if he does not get what he wants—if he does not find out the truth—he will be wearing, he is sure, a cuckold's horns. So he must not fail. He has to be even more careful than Falstaff. He has to win Falstaff's confidence, to tempt him successfully, and to do this he has to have a plausible reason for being there. He must present the bribe, and Falstaff must take it. Once that happens they can go on to the next step.

So each man is playing a role, hiding something, and at the same time trying to find out something. Since each has to find out what the other is hiding, each has to watch the other like a hawk. The audience, who knows the truths behind all the lies in this scene, can prepare themselves to watch the manipulators manipulate. How are the roles to be played? What kind of help does Verdi give? He gives a great deal of help—in fact, he gives directions.

Their first tactic as this beat begins is pretended politeness. Ford's entrance is marked sostenuto, lo stesso movimento, and pp. It is gracious, polite, and gentle, almost apologetic, perhaps even slightly obsequious. Falstaff's reply echoes this. Each must ingratiate himself with the other: Ford must reassure Falstaff so that he'll take the bait, and Falstaff must reassure Ford so that he will give Falstaff the wine.

FORD	FORD
Signore, v'assista il cielo!	Sir, may Heaven assist you!

FALSTAFF	FALSTAFF
Assista voi pur, signore.	May it assist you also, Sir.

FORD	FORD
Io sono, davver, molto indiscreto,	I am, truly, very indiscreet,
E vi chiedo perdono,	And I beg your pardon,
Se, senza ceremonie,	If, without standing on ceremony,
Qui vengo e sprovveduto	I come here, also without
Di più lunghi preamboli.	Longer preambles.

FALSTAFF	FALSTAFF
Voi siete il benvenuto.	You are welcome.

Falstaff makes a movement of acceptance on the downbeat (the "-to" of "benvenuto" and the marking *lo stesso movimento*). The tempo does not change, but the articulation in the orchestra is completely different: the meter changes, suggesting, perhaps, that they have accomplished their first steps and can now move ahead. Now there are four and a half bars of no text. What happens during this time? Ford must figure out what he wants to say next, and Falstaff must find a way to move Ford along. What might their actions be? Do they stay standing? Does Falstaff gesture for Ford to take a seat? Whatever the actions are, each character must be attentive to the other. Ford might look at Falstaff to confirm that his politeness has worked, that he has Falstaff's attention; Falstaff might look at Ford to confirm that *his* politeness has worked, that Ford is going to move on to the next step. And so the first beat ends.

On the basis of what he sees, Ford feels confident enough to take his next step. He will deploy his second tactic—explaining who he is. He says:

In me vedete un uom	In me you see a man
Che' ha un'abbondanza grande	Who has great abundance
Degli agi della vita;	Of the comforts of life;
Un uom che spende e spande	A man who spends and squanders
Come più gli talenta	However he most cares to
Pur . . . pur di passar mattana.	So long . . . so long as his whim passes.
Io mi chiamo Fontana!	My name is Fountain!

Again the marking is *p*: gracious, polite, and gentle—about as nonthreatening as it could be. Then, on "pur" there's a change: it's marked *f*, as is the next phrase. Why? Perhaps because he wants Falstaff to know that he will do anything so long as it satisfies his needs. Will Falstaff take the bait? Ford must be very vigilant. Each time he tries a tactic, he has to find out whether Falstaff is taking the bait. How can he know how to continue if he is not aware of Falstaff's reaction? Equally, Falstaff must watch Ford carefully—he needs to know whether he is going to get his hands on the demijohn and whether he is going to find out why the demijohn is being offered. Each has to be cued by the other; each relies on what he sees in the other for his next step.

The care with which Ford chooses his words has another purpose: to be suggestive, to imply. He says he is "un uom che spende e spande come più gli talenta pur . . . pur di passar mattana." This is full of suggestiveness; it carries a special meaning just below the surface that is essential for Falstaff to grasp. What Ford wants Falstaff to understand is: you will be the recipient of my largesse if you satisfy my need. He is not saying this directly, but implying it. How do we know that this is what he really means? We know that Ford is not in the least whimsical—especially not about his money (or his wife, or his reputation); he is the exact opposite of a big spender. The audience knows this from what it has seen of him in Act I; the singer playing Ford will know this from his total preparation. So in making this implied suggestion, Ford is going directly against what we know to be his character. Why is he doing this? There can only be one reason: because he thinks that to do so will lure Falstaff. There can be nothing extraneous in the scene; everything must relate to the objectives.

Falstaff shows that he gets the point:

Caro signor Fontana!	Dear Mister Fountain!
Voglio fare con voi	I want to become
Più ampia conoscenza.	Better acquainted with you.

The stage direction has Falstaff "andando a stringergli la mano con grande cordialità" (going to shake hands with great cordiality). His words too are full of suggestiveness: implied is "I understand exactly what you are saying." In the audience we might say, "Of course you do!" Perhaps Ford would think the same—but he must not say so to Falstaff. They shake hands and with this small climax the *second beat* is over.

So far the text is formal, polite—and completely insincere. What gives the scene its forward thrust is Ford's control. As we already know, Ford is not by nature a thoughtful or a patient man. He flies off the handle easily. What would his natural action be? Most likely, he would want to blurt out his question: are you seducing my wife? Falstaff, for his part, is wary, calculating, devious. His natural action would probably be to take the demijohn and begin drinking straight away, perhaps even to invite Ford to join him. There is nothing sincere in either man just now. Each has his own hidden agenda, which he must not reveal. Each is asking himself: What does he want? What is his plan? How can I find out?

After a brief interlude to get rid of Bardolfo and Pistola who are loitering near the door, the *third beat*, the next stage in Ford's entrapment of Falstaff, begins. As the music makes clear, Verdi helps him:

Sir John, m'infonde ardire	Sir John, a well-known folk saying
Un ben noto proverbio popolar:	Inspires me with boldness:
[fermata over "lar," then another	
with the direction "lunga pausa"]	
Si suol dire	It is generally said
Che l'oro apre ogni porta,	That gold opens every door,
Che l'oro è un talismano,	That gold is a talisman,
[fermata]	
Che l'oro vince tutto.	That gold conquers everything.
[fermata]	

The fermatas are telling. Obviously Ford can see the circumstances in which Falstaff is living: they are not luxurious. He can see Falstaff's size: it does not take a genius to realize that Falstaff is greedy. After each idea—gold opens doors, gold is good luck, gold gives power—he pauses. Why? Each idea should—he hopes—increase Falstaff's greed; each pause therefore gives Ford a chance to see if this is so, if his plan is working. Falstaff, who has his own plans, can react or not react—or he can acknowledge that each idea is correct, thereby buying a little time of his own and helping Ford move a little closer to revealing why he is there. He finally speaks: he caps Ford's description of gold's uses with an image of his own:

L'oro è un buon capitano	Gold is a good captain
Che marcia avanti.	Which marches ahead.

The image is appropriate for a knight, but it too has an implied meaning: it means that if Ford wants anything from Falstaff, he, Falstaff, expects to be paid first, before he does what he is asked to do. Gold marches ahead, not behind. So Falstaff too is helping move the scene along, to his own ends. Ford replies, again suggestively, committing himself to nothing but still turning up the heat:

Ebbene ...	Well then ...
Ho un sacco di monete	I have a sack of gold pieces
Qua, che mi pesa assai.	Here, which weighs me down greatly.
Sir John, se voi volete	Sir John, if you care
Aiutarmi a portarlo.	To help me carry it.

The effect of this is twofold: it gives Falstaff something concrete to see, and he has a chance to feel the sack's weight. The evidence—along with the temptation—is mounting. Perhaps because of this, Falstaff becomes almost direct:

Con gran piacer ...	With great pleasure ...
Non so, davver,	I don't know, really,
Per qual mio merito, Messere ...	Through what merit of mine, Sir ...

He needs more than ever to know what's going on. Ford tells him:

Ve lo dirò.	I will tell you.
C'è a Windsor una dama,	In Windsor there's a lady,
Bella e leggiadra molto,	Very beautiful and charming.
Si chiama Alice; è moglie	Her name is Alice; she's the wife
D'un certo Ford.	Of a certain Ford.

At the end of the first line, after "dirò," Verdi gives Ford a fermata. This is a significant pause: Ford is engaging Falstaff more and more. And it works: it makes Falstaff more and more interested. But it also makes him more careful, since it is precisely this Alice for whom he has his own plans. The music continues, and for two beats and a half neither says anything. Each watches the other. Falstaff speaks first. To provoke Ford, he says, "V'ascolto" (I'm listening to you). So Ford describes the situation. He loves her, but she does not love him; he writes to her, but she does not answer; he looks at her, but she ignores him; he seeks her, but she hides; he spends money, offers gifts, and contrives opportunities, but it is all in vain. He has been left alone, neglected and empty-handed, singing a madrigal. In response Falstaff begins singing his own madrigal, perhaps to see if Ford will join in, and he does. Falstaff sings "cantarellando scherzosamente" (softly, in a joking manner), as Verdi's stage directions have it:

FALSTAFF	FALSTAFF
"L'amor, l'amor	"Love, love

Che non ci dà mai tregue,
Finchè la vita strugge."

That never gives us respite,
Until life is consumed."

FORD
"... strugge."

FORD
"... consumed."

FALSTAFF
"È come l'ombra ..."

FALSTAFF
"It's like the shadow ..."

FORD
"... che chi fugge ..."

FORD
"... that when a man flees ..."

FALSTAFF
"... insegue ..."

FALSTAFF
"... it pursues him ..."

FORD
"E chi l'insegue ..."

FORD
"And when a man pursues it ..."

FALSTAFF
"... fugge."

FALSTAFF
"... it flees."

FORD
"L'amor!"

FORD
"Love!"

FALSTAFF
"L'amor!"

FALSTAFF
"Love!"

FORD
"L'amor!"

FORD
"Love!"

FALSTAFF
"L'amor!"

FALSTAFF
"Love!"

A contrast is enacted that reveals what each thinks about love—or seems to think. Ford plays the romantic, suffering because he cannot stop doing what gives him no satisfaction. Falstaff mocks this "tragic" view of love. An occasion is provided for some wary bonding: to make the madrigal work, they have to work together. But only for a moment: Falstaff interrupts Ford's attempt to get the madrigal going again by asking:

Essa non vi diè
Mai luogo a lusinghe?

She never gave you
Any occasion to flatter yourself?

and by finally coming directly to the point:

Ma infin,
Perchè v'aprite a me?

But, in short,
Why are you confiding in me?

Ford says he will now explain. He has succeeded in drawing Falstaff to him; he has made Falstaff ask him for something. So, for the moment, he has some power. This is the climax of the third beat. They are silent while the orchestra continues. Why? Because now Ford has either to make his final move—or not. He has to feel that the time is right for his announcement, that Falstaff is where he wants him to be. How will he know? The pause gives him yet another chance to study Falstaff. What he might also hope is that it's another chance for the knight's tension and expectation to increase. This is the end of the third beat.

Ford begins the fourth beat by flattering Falstaff. Perhaps he is picking up on the cynical attitudes Falstaff displayed in the madrigal; in any case, he is adding more bait to his trap. He then—but only because he feels the time is right—offers Falstaff his clincher: "Tutto il mio patrimonio!" (All my patrimony!) for just one small service:

Ma, in contraccambio, chiedo   But, in return, I ask
Che conquistiate Alice!   That you conquer Alice!

This is the climax of the scene. Ford has maneuvred Falstaff into feeling the weight of his very large sack of money. He has praised him and flattered him. He has gotten him into a position where it will be very difficult for Falstaff to turn down his request—however strange it might seem. Still, Falstaff has not entirely given up his critical faculties. He is amazed: "Strana ingiunzion!" (Strange command!), he says. So, quickly—before Falstaff can ask more questions—Ford begins to explain. His explanation must be credible, and it must depend on Falstaff's being so eager for cash, and so susceptible to being praised for his manly prowess, that he not will look too carefully at the proposition. Alice is so chaste, says Ford, that only if she is first conquered by a man—an experienced man, a real man—will Ford stand any kind of chance with her. The invitation is couched in terms that are bound to flatter Falstaff and will show Ford (this is his real agenda) what progress Falstaff has actually made with his wife. Ford finishes: "E allor . . . che ve ne par?" (And then . . . what do you think?). There is a fermata, a long one. What is it for? Is Sir John really thinking the proposition over? Is he dragging out the suspense to see what else Ford might be prepared to do? Is he asking himself whether this man can be serious? Or is he debating within himself what and how much to tell Ford about his rendezvous? Whatever choice Falstaff makes must be very clear to us. His actions will help make his choice clear. Finally he makes up his mind: first he accepts the money, then he tells Ford that "fra una mezz'ora sarà nelle mie braccia" (within half an hour she will be in my arms).

Ford explodes: "Chi?" (Who?). The stage direction is "come un urlo" (like a cry). He needs all his strength of will to control himself, to keep from giving himself away. But Falstaff misses this. Having made up his mind—to accept Fontana's commission, to take the gold and the wine, and to be "candid" with Fontana—he is calm. He does not pay attention, and thus he does not notice how intense Ford's response is. He indulges himself in an aria of triumph and then leaves to finish getting ready to meet Alice. His aria is full of bragging, insults, and mockery; its target is the soon-to-be-cuckolded husband of Alice. He has no idea that this is who is standing directly before him:

Il diavolo se lo porti	The devil take him
All'inferno con Menelao suo avolo!	To hell with Menelaus, his ancestor!
Quel tanghero, quel tanghero!	That boor! That boor!
Vedrai, vedrai, vedrai!	You'll see, you'll see, you'll see,
Vedrai, vedrai!	You'll see, you'll see!
Te lo cornifico netto, netto!	I'll cuckold him neatly, neatly!
Se mi frastorna	If he disturbs me
Gli sparo una girandola	I'll fire a Catherine wheel
Di botte sulle corna!	Of blows on his horns!
Quel messer Ford è un bue,	That Master Ford is an ox,
Un bue, vedrai, ecc.	An ox, you'll see, etc.
Ma è tardi.	But it's late.
Aspettami qua.	Wait for me here.
Vado a farmi bello.	I'm going to make myself handsome.

There is no subtext, no hidden agenda here: it is all plain. The aria goes from *ff* to *pp* to *f*, and so on; it is full of crescendos and decrescendos. Why does he revel in his expected triumph over a man he does not know? Is it not because he is so full of himself, and because for the moment he has an audience? After all, within a single hour he has managed to win a meeting with Alice, with all that that implies to him: sex with the lady, access to her husband's money. On top of that, here is this man, Fontana, offering him a demijohn of wine and a sack full of more money, with evidently no risk, and all for the purpose of asking Falstaff to do what he was going to do anyway. Why would he not he feel triumphant? At the end, reminded of the time, Falstaff can safely leave, having achieved his intention of finding out what Fontana wants. He can now return to his original objective: to get ready to visit Alice.

Needless to say, Ford is not feeling triumphant, even though he has gotten what he entered the scene to get: information. He now knows for sure that he is about to be betrayed. His aria, sung while Falstaff is offstage, is, like Falstaff's, entirely lacking in subtexts or hidden agendas: it is Ford at his most direct, most raw.

Falstaff returns, prancing, showing off his clothes, his body, his charm. The scene is over. Each man must now go on to his next objective. Both are polite, but both are seething, Ford with jealousy and rage, Falstaff with amorous expectation. Nonetheless, they play a small scene of harmonious insincerity: After you! No, after you, I insist! Each thinks he has gotten what he wanted. Only the audience, who has known the truth throughout the entire scene, knows what has really happened and what each will likely get in the end.

The scene as written is full of dramatic power and insight. But it will only come fully to life if Falstaff and Ford are able to use the scene's hidden agendas, beats, silences, and opportunities for watchfulness.

Part of the scene's power comes from the fact that the beats are so clear. Together, they constitute a ladder. Once one step has been achieved, the next can be mounted, and then the next, and so on until the action reaches its peak. Each step on this ladder is a separate beat—including the fall from the top that Ford experiences while Falstaff is offstage primping, when he can fully express his anguish. Breaking down the scene into beats helps the singers understand the way its action moves. It helps the director, too, since it is his job to make sure the scene keeps its shape and movement. Watching the singers rehearse, he has to see to it that the beats are clearly defined and that the transitions between them are clear. His eyes are our eyes here: it is up to him to ensure that we in the audience will be able to follow the action precisely.

The action of each beat is helped by Verdi's carefully plotted silences. The fermatas, which increase tension, are an aspect of Verdi's—and the character's—tactics for building suspense. The outcome of each beat is always in doubt until Falstaff agrees. Once he does so, a new beat is established in which Ford has new information; this he must digest before he can act upon it.

Hidden agendas, beats, and silences together signify a greater-than-usual need for the singers to watch each other. While no singer should ever *not* actively listen to the character with whom he's sharing a dialogue, the need for watchfulness is particularly intense in this scene. Any response that either Ford or Falstaff may make to the other must be a direct reply to the speech that stimulated it. In this high-stakes game, for either character to miss a clue could lead to failure.

If the scene is not shaped and managed successfully, its power will be greatly diminished. Falstaff's and Ford's arias will become just exercises in musical bravado or agitation; they will not be grounded in believable human behavior. And the audience, who knows enough of the truth to want to experience the full human, emotional power of the scene, will be cheated. Attention to the scene's hidden agendas, its beats, its silences, and its characters' watchfulness will help raise the stakes for the audience, will lead them to respond to the rising tensions in the scene. Given the amount of care that Verdi and his librettist, Arrigo Boito, plainly gave to shaping it, any less care on the part of the singers would cheat them as well.

Playing in a Crowd: Rossini, *L'italiana in Algeri*, Act I, Scenes 11–13

The nineteenth-century English poet and essayist Leigh Hunt, who liked Rossini's operas, wrote about him: "The author seems to delight in expressing a precipitate and multitudinous mirth; and sometimes works up and torments a passage, and pours in instrument upon instrument, till orchestra and singers all appear drunk with uproariousness, and ready to die on the spot" (Hunt, quoted in Osborne 2007, p. 86). But music can intoxicate only if it is played very carefully, with a complete absence of intoxication on the part of the players. That is a central paradox in the arts: only by means of the most rigorous discipline do transports occur.

And it points, in turn, to a real challenge in the staging of scenes that involve groups of people: the need for clarity and precision. Unless each actor in the group knows precisely why he or she is there and what the character wants, his or her actions cannot be clear; if a performer's actions are not clear, audiences will not know what they are watching or why. They will see a confused crowd, not an excited one.

This is mostly a director's problem, since it is he or she who has the overall control: it is up to the director to stage the scene—within the world he or she has created for the opera—so that an audience can see each character as distinct and understand how each contributes to the scene's overall action. But singers also have responsibilities: they have to take special care to make their characters' actions sharp and focused and not let them be blurred by generalized or empty gestures; they also have to respect the demands of the whole scene and not try to get special attention by mugging and hamming.

Rossini loved ensembles, as the passage from Leigh Hunt suggests, and he wrote very clear and precise music for them. *L'italiana in Algeri* is one of his earlier operas: it was written in only twenty-seven days in 1813, when he was twenty-one, and produced the same year. It is an opera that is known for its ensembles, especially the final scenes of the first act, which rise to a peak of music and singing—and acting—as the stage fills up with characters and the action progresses to its climax, bringing down the curtain. Important things happen in these scenes. The characters are not there just to fill out the music, and we in the audience have to see these things happen and understand them. If we cannot, the action will not make sense. And then the music will not be music; it will just be noise.

The opera is about separated lovers who are able in the end to come together, and especially about the cleverness of the heroine, Isabella—the Italian girl of the title—in arranging matters. It takes place mostly in the palace of Mustafà, the bey of Algiers. It is Mustafà who is the opera's major impediment and upon whom Isabella has to expend most of her ingenuity. He has decided that he is tired of his wife, Elvira; in fact, he is tired of all the women in his harem. What he wants, he thinks, is an Italian woman. He has some reason for thinking them special, as we will see. He has decided to divorce Elvira and marry her to his favorite slave, Lindoro. Lindoro, we learn, is a young Italian who has been separated (we don't know how) from his true love, who of course is Isabella. Conveniently, a passing ship is wrecked on a nearby coast; Haly (who is the captain of Mustafà's corsairs) and his men rescue the survivors, among whom are—conveniently—Isabella and her traveling companion, Taddeo. Isabella has been searching for Lindoro, helped by Taddeo, who unfortunately has begun to fall in love with her (which is something else she has to handle). Mustafà's excitement at the news of the arrival of an Italian girl is extreme. The final scenes of the first act show their meeting and impart new information as well. These scenes are not only crowded with people and incident, but are also complicated by a very Rossinian device: the use of asides. Two kinds of aside occur in these scenes: the aside to oneself, in which a character speaks his or her thoughts aloud in order to create the impression that we are overhearing what is going on inside his or her mind; and the aside in which a character speaks directly to the audience, not to other characters or to himself or herself. Making these levels of action clear for an audience requires organization and discipline.

First, Mustafà. He is coming from a lifetime of being able to successfully organize reality for himself; now, as always, it seems as if he is going to get what he wants. What does this mean? Well, he is an absolute ruler, with the power of life and death over all his subjects—which is to say, over everyone in the opera. As he tells Haly, who tries to object when Mustafà orders him to find him an Italian girl: "Se fra sei giorni non me la trovi, e segui a far lo scaltro, io ti faccio impalar" (If within six days you don't find her for me, and continue to play the clever one, I shall have you impaled). He wants Haly to

John Del Carlo, right, as Mustafà in a 1998 San Diego Opera production of L'italiana in Algeri. *(Photo by Ken Howard)*

do this because, as he says, he is so "sazio io son di questa moglie, che non ne posso più" (tired I am of this wife, that I cannot stand her any longer). Nor is he interested in the women of his harem: "Tante carezze, tante smorfie non son di gusto mio" (So many caresses, such [girlish] poutings are not to my taste). Then he tells us why he wants an Italian girl: "Ho una gran voglia d'aver una di quelle Signorine, che dan martello a tanti cicisbei" (I have a great desire to have one of those signorinas who give the hammer [make life miserable] to so many suitors). In other words, he has convinced himself he wants a woman who is a challenge, someone on whom he can test his mettle, someone he can master; his wife, Elvira, on the other hand, seems to want what we might today call a "relationship," something that holds no interest for Mustafà. Absolute though he may be, he is evidently not a monster unless he has to be: even though wants to get rid of his wife, he feels some concern for her, which is why he is not simply going to have her killed; instead, he is going to give her to his favorite slave, Lindoro, and send them both away to Italy. In any case, the fates seem to be once again bringing his wishes true: a vessel has been wrecked on his coast and on the vessel is Isabella, a genuine Italian girl. So where Mustafà is coming from is the belief that he really can have exactly what he wants. With this belief, we could say, he is puffed up. He's going to his great hall to "receive" Isabella; he wants everyone to be there to see his success at dealing with this Italian girl:

Or mi tengo da più del gran Sultano	Now I can regard myself as more than a great Sultan.
Presto: tutto s'aduni il mio serraglio nella sala maggior. Ivi la bella riceverò . . . ah! ah!	Quickly, let my whole harem assemble in the great hall. There the beauty I will receive. ha! ha!
Cari galanti, vi vorrei tutti quanti presenti al mio trionfi. . . .	Dear gallants, I'd like you, all of you, Present at my triumph. . . .
. . . .	. . . .
Con questa Signorina me la voglio goder. E agli uomini tutti ogg'insegnar io voglio di queste belle a calpestar l'orgoglio.	With this Signorina I want to have a good time. And to all men, today I wish to teach how to trample the pride of these beauties.

In his view there are no blocks to his getting what he wants, not since Elvira has been removed. There is a challenge, the Italian girl, who might try to resist him, but he is aroused and confident; he can only imagine "trionfi," and in fact a certain amount of resistance seems to be what he is looking forward to. Any impediment will be easy to deal with just as he has always dealt with impediments: by dismissing them or mastering them. Which is how he conceives of Isabella—as someone to be mastered. And so we see him at the beginning of scene 10 (the first scene of the finale): seated in his audience hall, surrounded by the women of his harem and a Chorus of Eunuchs, ready to display his mastery and be applauded.

At this point Isabella enters. As usual, she has been managing some tricky situations. She has been searching for her lover without having the least idea of where he is, she has been shipwrecked, and she has had to deal with a traveling companion, Taddeo, who wants more from her than she wants him to have. She has not found her lover—not yet—but she has survived the shipwreck, and she has managed both to make her position clear to Taddeo and still keep his support. She has heard about the bey and the dangers he represents and is entirely sanguine about him: "Non ci pensar per ora, Sarà quel che sarà" (Don't think about it for now, It will be what it will be). She is going to meet Mustafà, and she wants what she has always wanted: to find her lover, Lindoro. The usual fate of an attractive European woman shipwrecked on the coast of Algiers in the early 1800s would be to find herself part of a seraglio. So what might prevent her from finding Lindoro is the bey himself. As we have seen, Isabella is very cool (we saw this in her first scene with Haly's forces, in the aria "Cruda sorte"). She does not waste energy worrying over things: "Sarà quel che sarà." She has enough confidence in her own powers to face whatever will come.

What we have, then, is a set-up for the collision of two fully confident people. Out of such collisions can come comedy, especially if one of the people is overconfident. The first words belong to the chorus:

Viva, viva il flagel delle donne,	Long live the scourge of women,
Che di tigri le cangia in agnelle.	Who from tigresses changes them into ewes.
Chi non sa soggiogar queste belle	Whoever does not know how to subdue these beauties
Venga a scuola dal gran Mustafà.	Let him come to the school of the great Mustafà.

The Chorus of Eunuchs is well trained: they know how to support Mustafà's inflation. Isabella enters in scene 11. She is the first person to speak, and she rapidly pricks Mustafà's balloon:

(Oh! che muso, che figura! . . . Quali occhiate! . . . .Ho inteso tutto.	(Oh! What an ugly face, what a sight! . . . What leering! . . . I understand everything.

| Del mio colpo or son sicura. | Of my effect now I am sure. |
| Sta' a veder quel ch'io so far.) | Let me see what I can do.) |

In the libretto her speech is in parentheses, so the words are not being spoken to Mustafà. That is obvious: Mustafà may be a fool, but he can be dangerous. Isabella is careful; she knows what power he has. So to whom is she speaking? To herself? To the audience? If to herself, what she says represents her own thoughts; it is an aside to herself, the thoughts in her own mind; if to the audience, it is the traditional aside, which is in its own way a special kind of interaction with the audience. (An aside can also be to another character.) Each kind of speech will lead to a different kind of action. If Isabella is speaking to herself, she will show that by focusing on the thought and directing the line toward herself; if she is speaking to us in the audience, she will want to make eye contact with us. Whichever choice is made, Isabella must be seen by the audience—*not* by Mustafà—to make the discovery that Mustafà is a lecherous fool, is therefore someone she can handle. Mustafà's words confirm her judgment: all he can think about are her visible attributes:

(Oh! che pezzo da Sultano!	(Oh! What a tidbit fit for a sultan!
Bella taglia! . . . Viso strano . . .	Beautiful figure! . . . Face unusual . . .
Ah! m'incanta . . .	Ah! she enchants me . . . I'm already
m'innamora	in love.
Ma convien dissimular.)	But I'd better play the disinterested one.)

Mustafà's speech, like Isabella's, is spoken to himself. However, though she does not hear what he says, Isabella is very well aware of what is going on in Mustafà's mind, since his actions have already revealed his intentions. So, speaking directly to him, she offers her bait:

Maltrattata dalla sorte,	Ill-treated by fate
Condennata alle ritorte . . .	Condemned to chains . . .
Ah, voi solo, o mio diletto,	Ah, you alone, oh my beloved,
Mi potete consolar.	Can console me.

What she shows him, apart from her attractive self (enhanced by a respectful curtsy and inviting décolletage), is submission and vulnerability: only he has the power to "console" her. The Italian verb *consolare* carries the connotation of giving comfort, perhaps even sexual comfort. This shows Mustafà what he wants to see: that she already, after just a few minutes together, recognizes him as a master. Since he is not thinking, being entirely the prisoner of his libido, it seems clear to him that he has already won.

The duet that follows shows them again speaking to themselves, reveling in their separate understandings:

MUSTAFÀ
(Mi saltella il cor nel petto,
Che dolcezza di parlar!)

MUSTAFÀ
(My heart leaps in my breast.
How sweet is her speech!)

ISABELLA
(In gabbia è già il merlotto,
Nè più mi può scappar!)

ISABELLA
(The big fool is already entrapped,
And he can't escape from me now!)

MUSTAFÀ
(Io son già caldo e cotto
Nè più mi so frenar.)

MUSTAFÀ
(I am already on fire and in love,
No more can I contain myself.)

What do we in the audience see, as we listen to this? Is either of them aware of what the other is saying? Well, Mustafà's thoughts are not obscure to Isabella because she is able to use her brain; it is what she is thinking that Mustafà does not get, because for the moment he cannot. It is he who is caught up in a make-believe world, the world of pure wish fulfillment; by contrast, Isabella's inner life remains hidden. And that's how she is able to manage creatures such as Mustafà.

Into the midst of this comes Taddeo, trying to escape from Haly, to begin scene 12. They are not as dominant as Isabella, but Taddeo and Haly are still part of the scene. They cannot just occupy the stage; they have to know who they are and what they want so that their actions, in the midst of this large ensemble, can be clear to us in the audience. Taddeo has been picked up at the same time as Isabella by Haly's men; not being an Italian girl, however, he has been designated for execution. He wants to see the boss around here—Mustafà—in order to complain about his treatment, but naturally he would prefer to keep his head. Haly, or someone like him, might try to keep him from entering the hall, yet by sheer force of willpower he manages to get in, dragging Haly behind him. In itself this is comic, since in the real world it would be must unlikely for a prisoner to force his way into the main audience chamber of a figure such as Mustafà. What we are being shown is the equivalent of the annoying tourist who wants to complain to the hotel manager about his room. There is laughter to be won here, not by mugging or hamming, but simply by playing the moment for what it is: a reversal of expectations.

Haly has managed, miraculously, to do what he was ordered to do: find his master an Italian girl. He has been taking care of the other survivors of the shipwreck, including Taddeo, trying to prevent this obstinate prisoner from breaking in on his master. He wants to do his job, to not annoy his master, and to avoid impalement. Taddeo is proving to more of a handful than he had expected. So Haly is frustrated, annoyed, and probably a little frightened—if he cannot control this irritating man, how good is he at his job? He tries to explain: "Signor, quello sguajato . . ." (My lord, this coarse fellow . . .), he says, but Mustafà interrupts: "Sia subito impalato" (Must immediately be impaled). Luckily, Taddeo gets some help from Isabella. Taddeo's appearance is a small challenge to her: Mustafà must not get the idea Taddeo would like to be her lover (she must always keep in mind that the bey has absolute power within his world), so she has to find an explanation for his presence. Thinking fast, she says, "Egli è mio zio" (He is my uncle), so Mustafà will see he is not a rival and let him go. When he does this, Isabella says to him insinuatingly, "Caro, capisco adesso che voi sapete amar" (My dear, I understand now that you know how to love). Well, love has nothing to do with it; it is all about inflammation, and her words have exactly that effect on Mustafà: "Non so che dir, me stesso, cara, mi fai scordar" (I don't know what to say, myself, dearest, you make me lose my head). Where does all this *caro/cara* stuff come from? Are Mustafà and Isabella already so intimate? Of course not, except where it counts: in Mustafà's imagination. This Isabella understands very well. Her manipulation of Mustafà seems right now to be a success.

But there is a new scene and a new challenge. Onto the stage come Mustafà's dismissed wife, Elvira; her servant, Zulma; and the man to whom Mustafà has given Elvira, Lindoro. They have come to say good-bye. (For clarity, we will do the questions for each.)

	ELVIRA	LINDORO	ZULMA
From where?	Dismissed by M; being sent to Italy to marry L	Is favorite of M; was chosen by M to take E to Italy (gaining his freedom) and marry her, plus have lots of cash	Is E's confidante; listens to her, is sympathetic to her
To where?	To say goodbye to M	To say goodbye to M	With E, to say goodbye to M
Wants what?	Still loves M, even though she knows he is eager for an Italian girl; wants to try to change his mind	Wants to just get on boat and get away as fast as possible	So far as we know, to continue her role, keep her job; or perhaps she is in love with Haly
Blocked by?	M's focus on I; he won't want to hear from E	Possibility M will come up with something new that would keep him from being sent away	Possibility M will come up with something that would prevent this
Overcomes how?	Likely can't overcome	L will try to get E and Z out of there quickly	Will try to stay

We can see that for each of these three, the stakes are high, though very different. Although Elvira wants to have one last go at Mustafà, Lindoro wants to get away as fast as he can, and Zulma wants to stay. How will the singers show this? There is not much time, and a lot is happening onstage, so their actions must be extremely well focused and accurate.

As they enter and move toward Mustafà, saying their farewells, they are unseen by Isabella, who is busy comforting Taddeo. Finally she turns back to Mustafà, at exactly the moment when Lindoro and the others, having been dismissed, move toward their exit. At just this moment, Isabella and Lindoro catch sight of each other and we enter another world—the world of spoken thoughts, or asides to oneself, not a world where thoughts are audible to the others. This is what they say inside their own minds:

ISABELLA
(O ciel!)

ISABELLA
(Oh Heaven!)

LINDORO
(Che miro!)

LINDORO
(What do I see!)

ISABELLA
(Sogno?)

ISABELLA
(Am I dreaming?)

LINDORO
(Deliro? Quest'è Isabella!)

LINDORO
(Am I delirious? That is Isabella!)

ISABELLA
(Quest'è Lindoro!)

ISABELLA
(That is Lindoro!)

LINDORO
(Io gelo.)

LINDORO
(I am turned to ice.)

ISABELLA
(Io palpito.)

ISABELLA
(My heart is pounding.)

BOTH
(Che mai sarà?
Amore, aiutami per carità.)

BOTH
(Whatever will happen?
Love, help for pity's sake!)

Each is amazed, and each gives voice to that amazement. Each grapples with what he or she is looking at. But to no one else—and not at all to each other—do they speak. Why not? Because each has a special relationship with Mustafà that would be jeopardized if he were to realize who each really was. If they were to speak their thoughts aloud, it would mean their deaths.

However, everyone else can *see* that Isabella and Lindoro are stupefied.

MUSTAFÀ, ELVIRA,	MUSTAFÀ, ELVIRA,
ZULMA, HALY	ZULMA, HALY
(Confusi e stupidi, incerti	(Confused and bewildered, uncertain
pendono;	they stand;
Non so comprendere tal novità.)	I can't understand this new situation.)

Even though this group says the same words, none of them are speaking to each other; are they all thinking the same thing? In naturalistic terms, this would be unlikely; in the terms given by the opera, it is not. This has implications for how they might behave—like puppets, perhaps? In comedy, it is the characters who are least adaptable who most resemble automatons, who are fixed in their behavior and ambitions. And most comic characters, adaptable or not, have moments of this kind of fixity. Their sentiments are repeated several times, as are the next thoughts of Isabella and Lindoro:

ISABELLA, LINDORO	ISABELLA, LINDORO
(Oh, Dio, che fulmine! non so	(Oh God, what a thunderbolt, I don't
rispondere.	know how to react.
Amore, aiutami per carità.)	Love, help me for mercy's sake.)

A scene as complicated as this one needs a director who can help clarify the actions of each character. Aside from the blocking, the director should help each character define his or her attitudes within each line.

The director should work to illuminate the music. For example, in the opening of the septet, as Mustafà, Elvira, Zulma, and Haly are looking at Lindoro and Isabella and wondering what is going on, it is Mustafà who has the first line: "Confusi e stupidi incerti pendono; Non so comprendere tal novità." The first part of the line is isolated; the other characters join in only on "comprendere," the third-to-last word. Two bars later, Lindoro enters with his line: "Oh! Dio, che fulmine! Non so comprendere, amore aiutami per carità." But the words "che fulmine! Non so comprendere, amore" are isolated. The director must keep the focus on the solo line. In this scene, it is these two characters who have these two repeated solo lines. By isolating them visually for these lines and emphasizing the repetitions and the inability of the characters to move beyond the situation, the director can keep the focus of the scene on the characters.

Even Taddeo has something to say: characteristically, he is not part of either group, but off by himself, sulking:

TADDEO	TADDEO
(Oh, Dio, che fremito! oh Dio, che	(Oh, God, what agitation! Oh, God,
spasimo!	what agony!
Che brutto muso fa Mustafà.)	What an ugly scowl has Mustafà.)

This ensemble beat stops. The tempo changes, and we come back to "reality." The dialogue that follows is, for what it shows about the distribution of power among the characters onstage, the center of the scene.

ISABELLA
Dite, chi è quella femmina?

ISABELLA
Say, who is that woman?

MUSTAFÀ
Fu sino ad or mia moglie.

MUSTAFÀ
She was till now my wife.

ISABELLA
Ed or? . . .

ISABELLA
And now? . . .

MUSTAFÀ
Il nostro vincolo, cara,
Per te si scioglie:
Questi che fu mio schiavo
Si dee con lei sposar.

MUSTAFÀ
Our ties, my dear,
For you are being dissolved:
This man, who was my slave,
Must with her be married.

ISABELLA
Col discacciar la moglie
Da me sperate amore?
Questi costumi barbari
Io vi far`o cangiar.
Resti con voi la sposa . . .

ISABELLA
By discarding your wife
From me you hope for love?
These barbarous customs
I shall make you change.
Let your wife stay with you . . .

MUSTAFÀ
Ma questa non è cosa . . .

MUSTAFÀ
But this is not what . . .

ISABELLA
Resti colui
   mio schiavo.

ISABELLA
And let that man remain
   as my slave.

MUSTAFÀ
Ma questo non può star.

MUSTAFÀ
But this cannot be.

ISABELLA
Andate dunque al diavolo,
Voi non sapete amar.

ISABELLA
Go then to the devil,
You don't know how to love.

MUSTAFÀ
Ah! no . . . M'ascolta . . . acchetati . . .
(Ah! costei mi fa impazzar.)

MUSTAFÀ
Ah no! . . . Listen . . . calm down . . .
(Ah! She drives me crazy!)

Isabella, having sized up Mustafà, can challenge him, even manipulate him. Still, she is taking a big risk. She has no idea what the outcome of her challenge will be. What she knows about Mustafà is not only that he is a libidinous fool; she also knows he is irrational, changeable, and dangerous. So with each step she takes, she must be very careful to observe his reactions to her statements and her actions. She can grow bolder—and she certainly does—but she must never feel completely secure, never smug. In fact, the only time in the opera when she can feel fully secure is in the finale of Act II, when Mustafà has taken Elvira back and she and Lindoro are on their way home. At any rate, with her challenge and Mustafà's discombobulation, the world changes again, out of reality and back into full-blown special asides. It is a world of short-circuits and amazement, perhaps not unlike what goes on in Mustafà's head. First Elvira, Zulma, and Lindoro respond, laughing, but not so that Mustafà can see them, and not for the same reasons; again, these are asides to themselves, actions occurring within their own minds. They have the same words because they are on the same wavelength.

(Ah! Di leone in asino Lo fe' costei cangiar.)	(Ah! From a lion into an ass, That girl made him change.)

Then Taddeo, Mustafà himself, Haly, and even Isabella join in. This is what happens, without the repeats:

TADDEO, MUSTAFÀ, ELVIRA, ZULMA, ISABELLA, LINDORO, HALY	TADDEO, MUSTAFÀ, ELVIRA, ZULMA, ISABELLA, LINDORO, HALY
Va sossopra il mio cervello Sbalordito in tanti imbrogli; Qual vascel fra l'onde e i scogli Io sto/ei sta presso a naufragar.	It's going topsy-turvy my brain Bewildered in so much confusion; Like a vessel amid waves and reefs I am/he is about to founder.

The chorus has the same observations:

CORO	CHORUS
Va sossopra il suo cervello Ei sta presso a naufragar.	It's going topsy-turvy his brain He is about to founder.

Then the rest then have their say, alone and in groups:

ELVIRA, ISABELLA, ZULMA	ELVIRA, ISABELLA, ZULMA
Nella testa ho un campanello Che suonando fa din din.	In my head I have a bell That ringing goes ding ding.

LINDORO, HALY	LINDORO, HALY
Nella testa un gran martello Mi percuote e fa tac tà.	In my head a big hammer Beats on me and goes bang bang.

<table>
<tr><td>

TADDEO
Sono come una cornacchia
Che spennata fa crà crà.

MUSTAFÀ
Come scoppio di cannone
La mia testa fa bum bum.

</td><td>

TADDEO
I am like a crow
That plucked goes caw caw.

MUSTAFÀ
Like a shot from a cannon
My head goes boom boom.

</td></tr>
</table>

It is very busy. No one expects his or her words to reach the audience—who could make them out in all this exuberance?

To work, the scene has to be choreographed. Nothing about it is naturalistic. Nonetheless, although we do not know what anyone is saying, we must be clear about what each is thinking. Therefore, it is the director who must ensure that the singers and the characters "play together." If the director sets the scene so that all the characters are doing the same movements, then each singer must find for his or her character the particular gesture or movement that expresses bewilderment. Mustafà's bewilderment will be different from Haly's, which will not be the same as Lindoro's, and so on. If the scene is set so that each character makes the same gesture on the same line, then each gesture or action must be unique to the character. Rossini's music is extraordinarily precise, and so must each singer's gesture be.

Given the director's role, this may sound like a different kind of "playing together." But it is not. It depends as much as any other scene on each performer's knowing why his or her character is in the scene and what that character wants. Its success depends, as does that of any other scene, on each character's ability to pay attention to other characters, to interact.

5

Problem Arias

ALL ARIAS ARE CHALLENGES. For the singer: to know the music and words; to be in technical control of voice, breathing, and rhythm; to understand why the character must sing this aria at this moment; to know clearly to whom he or she is singing (another character? the audience? God? him- or herself?); to project words, music, and character to everyone in the hall; and to make it all look and sound natural. For the director: to create a world within which the action of the opera—and the aria—can take place; to be clear about the objectives and intentions of the character singing the aria; to understand how this character's actions are interwoven with the actions of other characters; and to be sure that the audience can clearly follow it all. For the audience: to respond not only to the beauty and power of the aria, but to its role in the action of the whole.

But some arias are problems as well. Here are three kinds of problem aria: the aria that is been put into an opera after it has been completed; the aria that invites emoting at the expense of character development or action; and, finally, the famously difficult da capo aria. Each of these problems has its own solution.

The Dropped-In Aria: Gounod, *Faust*, Act II, Scene 2

The plot is where the action is. An aria does not have the luxury of not advancing it. To drop an aria into the plot after the opera has been completed can have the effect of stopping or confusing the action. That is what can happen in Gounod's *Faust* with Valentin's famous aria "Avant de quitter ces lieux" (Before I leave this place).

Faust had its premier in 1859, at the Théâtre Lyrique in Paris. From the beginning, it was a success; in fact, throughout the last third of the nineteenth century it was one of the most-performed operas in the world. Its popularity drew the ire of some: George Bernard Shaw said that the typical critic had to spend "about ten years out of every twelve of his life listening to *Faust*. . . . I am far from sure that my eyesight has not been damaged by protracted contemplation of the scarlet red coat and red limelight of Mephistopheles."

Nonetheless, it did not emerge fully formed from its creator's mind. Gounod had revised the work extensively before its premier, cutting his original score by almost one-third, and he continued to revise it for about ten years afterward. It was only in 1863, four years after the premier, that he introduced the aria "Avant de quitter ces lieux" for the young English baritone Charles Santley, who had sung the role of Valentin in London. He placed it in the second scene of Act II, in the midst of celebrations of the Kermesse (the Easter fair), and it became one of the most beloved of the opera's many loved arias. Why did Gounod add the aria where he did? How can a director and singer make this dropped-in piece fit naturally into the opera's action?

The opera's story is well-known. It is based on the first part of Goethe's dramatic poem *Faust*, itself drawn, like Marlowe's play *Doctor Faustus*, from traditional material having to do with the figure of a wandering magician or polymath from the early sixteenth century. Gounod got to know Goethe's play in a French translation by Gérard de Nerval; it made a powerful impression on him, and he began right away (in the early 1840s, while he was still a student in Rome) drafting musical ideas for a potential opera. This translation and the play developed from it by Michel Carré *(Faust et Marguerite)* were the source of the libretto, which was written by Carré's partner Jules Barbier, with some help from Carré himself.

Faust is one of the great heroic obsessives of Western literature. His desire is boundless: to know, and to be, everything. Just as boundless is his despair at the feeling that he's failed. The opera begins with his cry of frustration, "Rien!" (Nothing!):

Rien!	Nothing!
En vain j'interroge, en mon ardente veille	In vain, I question, through my fervent vigil
La nature et le Créateur;	Nature and the Creator;
Pas une voix ne glisse à mon oreille	No voice comes to whisper in my ear
Un mot consolateur!	A consoling word!
J'ai langui triste et solitaire	I have languished, sad and alone,
Sans pouvoir briser le lien	Powerless to break the chain
Qui m'attache encore à la terre!	That still binds me to this world!
Je ne vois rien! Je ne sais rien!	I see nothing! I know nothing!
Rien! Rien!	Nothing! Nothing!

In anguish, he reaches for poison. Just then groups of peasant girls and men pass by outside his window; their high spirits turn his misery into anger and defiance, so instead of killing himself he summons the devil, Méphistophélès. Asked what he wants, Faust says, "Je veux la jeunesse!" (I want youth!). What does Méphistophélès want in return? "Presque rien: ici, je suis à ton service, mais là-bas, tu serais au mien" (Hardly anything. Here I am at your service, but down there, you will be in mine). Méphistophélès calls up a vision of Marguerite, a beautiful and innocent village girl living with her brother, Valentin, who will soon head off to the wars; Faust eagerly seals the bond, and the action is under way.

With Méphistophélès' help, Faust seduces Marguerite, then leaves her. She gives birth to his child; Valentin returns, discovers what has happened to his sister, and fights with Faust; helped by Méphistophélès, Faust wounds him; as he lies dying, Valentin curses his sister. Méphistophélès takes Faust away into the mountains to celebrate Walpurgis Night, the Witches' Sabbath; at the end, a vision of Marguerite appears, with a red ribbon around her neck; Faust demands to be taken to her. She is in prison; in despair and madness she has killed the baby; she will be executed at dawn. Méphistophélès brings Faust to the prison; Faust pleads with her to escape with him, but she is terrified at the sight of Méphistophélès and stays where she is, praying for forgiveness. She dies; her soul rises to heaven; Faust is left below. For Marguerite, the innocent, there is something—redemption; Faust returns to his state of "rien," only this time the condition is permanent.

What Gounod cut a good deal of, in preparing *Faust* for its premier, was the role of Valentin. The only thing left of it was his appearance near the end of Act IV, where he fights with Faust and dies cursing Marguerite. So we can see that Gounod's insertion of Valentin into the second scene of Act II was an attempt to give the character, and the singer playing him, something more to do. The composer was pleased to do this for Santley, who was a much better singer than the baritone who had played the role in Paris. Still, Gounod seems not to have been entirely happy with the insertion: it was never included at the Théâtre Lyrique or at the Opéra in the nineteenth century, nor did it appear in French scores published in Gounod's lifetime. And he was right to be uneasy: Valentin's appearance in Act II does create problems. The aria is usually sung today, partly because it is so popular, and partly because to leave it out could make getting a singer for what is otherwise so brief a role difficult. So the singer and director have to find a way to solve the problematic entrance and aria of the Valentin scene.

If we look at the whole sequence of events in Act II, the reasons for Gounod's concern are clear. The scene opens on an Easter fair, the

Stephen Powell as Valentin in a 2004 Opera Company of Philadelphia production of Gounod's Faust. *(Photo by Kelly and Massa)*

Kermesse. Groups of students, soldiers, burghers, young girls, and matrons are enjoying themselves led by Wagner, a young student. The music is lively (it's marked *allegretto*), wine and beer flow, and each group has its own fun—the students and soldiers want to drink and chase girls; the burghers want to drink and complain about their wives; the girls want to be chased, maybe even caught; and the matrons think the girls are shameless though they might like to be chased themselves. Into the midst of this happy scene comes Valentin, holding up a small religious medallion; he has some conversation with Wagner and the others, he sings his aria, "Avant de quitter ces lieux" (Before I leave this place), and then Wagner himself begins an aria, a story about a rat and a cat. This is interrupted by Méphistophélès, who has his own aria, "Le veau d'or" (The golden calf), about the calf's great power and about Satan making everyone dance around it (the story comes from the book of Exodus). Everyone enjoys this, and they offer Méphistophélès some wine; he throws it away and makes better wine gush from the barrel on the inn's sign. He tells fortunes: Wagner, he says, will die in an attack; Siebel will never touch a flower without its withering; and Valentin will be killed by someone he, Méphistophélès, knows. He proposes a toast to Marguerite; Valentin challenges him; Méphistophélès draws a circle around himself that shatters Valentin's sword; Valentin holds up its hilt in the form of a cross; Méphistophélès draws back. The crowd leaves the stage as Méphistophélès salutes them, promising he will return. Faust appears; he wants to see Marguerite; the villagers continue their festival; Marguerite appears; Faust approaches her and is rebuffed; and the act ends with dancing and singing.

All of the scene's action concerns the fair, the entry of Méphistophélès, the games he plays with the students, and his dismissal. Its trajectory goes from the happily rowdy to the demonic, and the scene culminates with Faust's tentative approach to Marguerite. Valentin's appearance in the midst of this, holding his medallion, is at best a distraction. His first words are:

Ô sainte médaille,	O blessed medal,
Qui me viens de ma soeur	Which my sister gave me,
Au jour de la battaille	On the day of battle,
Pour écarter la mort,	To avoid death,
Reste là sur mon coeur!	Stay here on my heart!

This introduction of something so highly personal and emotional into such public festivities is unexpected and awkward. The awkwardness is clear from Wagner's uncertainty: he is not sure why Valentin is there or what he wants, so Valentin has to explain:

WAGNER
Ah! voici Valentin qui nous cherche
   sans doute!

WAGNER
Ah! Here is Valentin, who is looking for
   us, no doubt.

VALENTIN
Un dernier coup, messieurs, et
   mettons-nous en route!

VALENTIN
One last drink, gentlemen, and then we
   must march!

WAGNER
Qu'as-tu donc?
Quels regrets attristent nos adieux?

WAGNER
What is the matter?
What regrets sadden our farewells?

VALENTIN
Comme vous, pour longtemps, je vais
   quitter ces lieux;
J'y laisse Marguerite, et pour
Veiller sur elle, ma mère n'est plus là!

VALENTIN
Like you, I am leaving this place for a
   long time;
I leave Marguerite here, and my mother
Is not here anymore to watch over her!

SIEBEL
Plus d'un ami fidèle
Saura te remplacer à ses côtés!

SIEBEL
More than one faithful friend
Will take your place at her side!

VALENTIN (lui serrant la main)
Merci!

VALENTIN (shaking his hand)
Thank you!

SIEBEL
Sur moi tu peux compter!

SIEBEL
You can count on me!

LES ÉTUDIANTS
Compte sur nous aussi!

STUDENTS
Count on us too!

Since what Valentin has to say—what he wants—is so at variance with the action of the scene, it is a challenge for the singer to prepare to make his entrance.

For this, trying to do the usual analysis does not help. Valentine has been saying good-bye to his sister. But has he just come from his house? Has he been in the crowd all along? If he has, why hasn't Wagner or anyone else mentioned him? If he has just said good-bye to his sister, why isn't she here with him? Wouldn't she want to be? Wouldn't he want her to be? He enters holding his medallion. In fact, he is singing to his medallion (rhetorical device called an apostrophe); he says, "Ô sainte médaille," and holds it up so it can be seen. It seems that what he wants is to show off the medallion Marguerite has given him, a talisman he thinks will keep him safe in battle. But why would someone want to do something like this, especially in the midst of a village fair? We see that he is worried about Marguerite, who will be left on her own when he is gone. So evidently his objective is to make sure she'll be looked after while he is away. But isn't that a private matter to be settled at home? Why does he bring it here, to a public festival? And who is he asking for this protection? The same students who have been singing happily about wanting to drink and chase girls. If his objective is to get some protection for Marguerite, perhaps they will be too busy drinking and singing to notice him. Perhaps that is why he is holding up his medallion—to get their attention. And perhaps, too, that is why he is so intent on showing his credentials: that he is religious (the medal is "holy"), that he is brave (he is going to war), and that he is loved by his sister (she gave him the medal so that it could protect him). But we are still not sure; we still want to ask, Who is this guy?

Some of these questions can be answered, or partly answered, in Valentin's aria:

Avant de quitter ces lieux,	Before I leave this place,
Sol natal de mes aïeux,	The native land of my ancestors,
À toi, Seigneur et Roi des cieux,	To you, Lord and King of Heaven,
Ma soeur je confie.	I entrust my sister.
Daigne de tout danger	From every danger,
Toujours la protéger,	Always protect her,
Cette soeur si chérie.	My sister, who is so dear to me.
Délivré d'une triste pensée,	Freed from a sorrowful thought,
j'irai chercher la gloire au sein des ennemis,	I will go to seek glory amid the enemy,
Le premier, le plus brave, au fort de mêlée.	The first, the bravest, in the thick of the fight.
J'irai combattre pour mon pays.	I will go and fight for my country.
Et si, vers lui, Dieu me rappelle,	And if God should call me to him,
Je veillerai sur toi fidèle,	I shall watch over you, faithfully,
Ô Marguerite.	O Marguerite.
Avant de quitter ces lieux, *etc.*	Before I leave this place, *etc.*
Ô Roi des cieux, jette les yeux,	O King of Heaven, cast your eyes upon us
Protège Marguerite, Ô Roi des cieux.	And protect Marguerite, O King of Heaven.

The music is in three sections. The first is marked *moderato*, and is *legato* in its line; this is his address—a prayer?—to the holy medal. Then, when he sings "Délivré d'une triste pensée," the music changes dramatically: it is marked *un poco più animato*, a little more animated, and it takes on a quasi-military flavor; in this section he is thinking of himself as a hero, "le premier, le plus brave, au fort de la mêlée." Finally, as he imagines his death and sees himself looking down on Marguerite from heaven, the music changes again: it slows down a bit, *rallentando un poco*; it becomes prayerful again. And intensely emotional.

This is quite a performance: what we are seeing is the presentation of an idealized but entirely conventional person. This is not to say, necessarily, that he is insincere. However, because it all happens in public, we have to wonder what Valentin's motives are—why he wants to show himself this way. To help us see his character more clearly, we can look ahead to his next appearance, which is also his final one. In the second and third scenes of Act IV, when Valentin returns from the war, we see him eager to find Marguerite; we see Siebel begging him to be merciful (without explaining why) and trying to stop him from going into his house; finally we see him enter. Then, in the next scene, we see Méphistophélès and Faust approach, Faust wanting another meeting with Marguerite even though he has deserted her. Méphistophélès sings an ironic serenade, "Ne donne un baiser, ma mie, que la bague au doigt!" (Don't give a kiss, my love, until the ring is on your finger!), but it is Valentin, not Marguerite, who appears, having learned what has happened to her. He realizes that he is facing her seducer and challenges him to a duel:

Assez d'outrage, assez!	Enough of this outrage, enough!
À qui de vous dois-je demander compte	Which one of you must I call to account
De mon malheur et de ma honte?	For my misery and my disgrace?
Qui de vous deux doit	Which of you two must fall under the
tomber sous mes coups?	blows of my sword?

His words are revealing. What concerns him is his misfortune, his shame; there is no thought of what Marguerite is suffering. When he is defeated and dying, Marguerite appears—it is the first and only time we see them together. His final words to her are a curse:

Marguerite!	Marguerite!
Sois maudite!	Be cursed!
La mort t'attend sur ton grabat!	Death awaits you on your pallet!
Moi, je meurs de ta main et je tombe	I die by your hand and fall like
en soldat!	a soldier!
(Il meurt.)	(He dies.)

At no point does Valentin show sympathy for his sister; instead, what counts for him is his honor, his misfortune, and the fact that he is dying "en soldat." The entire scene, like Valentin's earlier one, occurs in public. What would he have said in private?

From this we learn two things about Valentin, both of which help us understand how to approach his first appearance in Act II. The first is that he is overwhelmingly concerned with appearances, with how his character and behavior are perceived. The second is that he has a great need to be seen in particular socially acceptable ways: as a faithful Christian, a devoted patriot, and a hero. It is as if he has no inner self; all his energies are absorbed in the presentation of a persona. With this in mind, it is possible to see how Valentin's appearance in Act II, scene 2 can be presented.

Two things are needed: some kind of link between the crowd and Valentin's dominant concern, and boldness. If Valentin is seen entering with Siebel and showing him the medallion, telling him about it, he has the link to the group and the introduction he needs for his aria. This does not alter the fact that his appearance changes the dynamic of the scene, but it does provide a transition; it makes the scene's action *seem* to be continuous. And because Valentin's aria is so public, it cannot be disguised; the whole group onstage hears it. Therefore he should sing it boldly; he should be who he is. He wants approval? Then he should seek the crowd's approval for what he believes himself to be. And once he has done that, he has gotten what he wants and can move on—to depart for the wars, to confront Méphistophélès, to whatever he has to do next.

The aria—and Valentin's appearance—are still problematic. But they can be made dramatic.

Another suggestion is one that I do not claim to have originated. We know that one of the passages Gounod cut before the opera's premier was a duet between Valentin and Marguerite in Act II. We do not know what it consisted of, but we can easily see its utility: it would have let us see their relationship in positive terms. As it is, we only get to see them together at the end of the fourth act, when they're already estranged. So why not put something positive back? At the beginning of Act III, which takes place in the garden outside Marguerite's house, Siebel enters to sing an aria, "Faites-lui mes aveux" (Confess to her for me). He is holding flowers that he wants to leave for her, and it is to them that he is singing. Why not have him joined by Wagner and some townspeople as they wait for Valentin to take his leave of his sister? In that context, the aria "Avant de quitter ces lieux" would make more sense, since we could see exactly the lieux that he was talking about. We could still see Siebel and the townspeople agreeing to take care of her. Most important, seeing Valentin and Marguerite together would establish their relationship. After Valentin sings his aria, he and the others could depart, Marguerite could go into her house, and Siebel could still sing his aria.

The Sentimental Aria: Gounod, *Faust*, Act III, Scene 4

When an opera's action stops, what do we in the audience do? We look around, we fidget and twist; our attention falls away from what is happening onstage. If the action stops because something beautiful is happening, a beautifully sung aria, we might not twitch, but we can still fall just as far away by simply losing ourselves in the wonder of the moment. The consequences are the same: we forget why the singer is singing what he has to sing, we ignore what has happened to bring him to this point, and we don't care where he has to go; we lose the drama.

Some arias encourage this. Some productions allow it to happen.

In Act III, scene 4 of *Faust*, the title character has a wonderful piece to sing when Méphistophélès brings him to Marguerite's garden. Méphistophélès leaves Faust there alone while he goes to get a casket of jewels with which to tempt her and prepare her to be seduced by Faust. (That he is successful will be seen two scenes later in her Jewel Song.) While Faust is alone, he has a chance to contemplate Marguerite's simple cottage and garden; what he sees opens him up to thoughts and reactions he has never had, nor expected to have. Gounod's cleverness in bringing these two innocents together—Faust and Marguerite—under the manipulation of Méphistophélès is what creates the opera's tragedy.

Faust's aria is wonderful. But it is also a challenge: not only is it vocally difficult, but it poses a risk for both singer and director that its beauty and vocal demands will cause him to forget to act and instead resort to emoting and posturing. Powerful things happen to Faust in the aria, and we in the audience need to see clearly what he discovers here as a preparation for what happens to him in the rest of the opera.

Quel trouble inconnu me pénètre?	What unknown turmoil pierces me?
Je sens l'amour s'emparer de mon être!	I sense that love takes hold of my whole being!
Ô Marguerite! à tes pieds me voici!	O Marguerite, here I am at your feet!
Salut! demeure chaste et pure, où se devine	Hail, chaste and pure dwelling, where one can feel
La présence d'une âme innocente et divine!	The presence of an innocent and holy soul.
Que de richesse en cette pauvreté!	What richness in this poverty!
En ce réduit, que de félicité!	In this humble abode, what happiness!
Ô nature, c'est là que tu la fis si belle!	O Nature, it is here where you made her beautiful!
C'est là que cette enfant a dormi sous ton aile,	It is here where this child slept under your wing,
A grandi sous tes yeux!	Grew up before your eyes!
Là que, de ton haleine enveloppant son âme,	Here, with your breath enveloping her soul,
Tu fis avec amour épanouir la femme	You lovingly made this angel of heaven

En cet ange des cieux!	Bloom into a woman!
C'est là! . . . oui . . . C'est là!	It is here . . . yes . . . here it is!
Salut! demeure chaste et pure, *etc.*	Hail, chaste and pure dwelling, *etc.*

The usual process of analysis is again helpful here. In terms of the larger action of the opera, Faust is coming from the state of despair we saw at the very beginning, in Act I, scene 1. He has spent his life as a scholar, isolated and apart from the world, and all that work has brought him is "Rien!"

J'ai langui triste et solitaire,	I have languished, sad and alone,
Sans pouvoir briser le lien	Powerless to break the chain
Qui m'attache encore à la terre!	That still binds me to this world!
Je ne vois rien! Je ne sais rien!	I see nothing! I know nothing!
Rien! Rien!	Nothing! Nothing!

When Méphistophélès asks him what he wants, he says no to riches, no to glory; what he wants, he cries, is "la jeunesse!" (youth!) What does this mean for him?

À moi les plaisirs,	I want pleasures,
Les jeunes maîtresses!	And also young ladies!
À moi leurs caresses!	I want their caresses!
À moi leurs désirs!	I want their desires!
À moi l'énergie	I want the energy
Des instincts puissants,	Of powerful instincts
Et la folle orgie	And the mad revelry
Du coeur et des sens!	Of the heart and the senses!
Ardente jeunesse,	Fervent youth,
À moi tes désirs,	I want your desires,
À moi ton ivresse,	I want your raptures,
À moi tes plaisirs!	I want your pleasures!

In other words, he wants abandon, freedom from the consciousness he has worked so hard to gain, rapture, trips in his very own *bateau ivre*. Méphistophélès tempts him with a vision of Marguerite; Faust, in a transport of wonder and desire, signs away his soul, and the action is under way. He meets Marguerite at the town fair; she rejects him; his passion is increased. Méphistophélès takes him to Marguerite's house; they see Siebel, who is in love with Marguerite and who leaves a bouquet of flowers at her door. Earlier, at the Kermesse, Méphistophélès had promised that any flower that Siebel touched would wither; Siebel has parried this by dipping his hand in holy water, and the flowers he picked have indeed survived. It is this that Méphistophélès will in turn counter with the casket of jewels, which he has gone to get. So, in immediate terms, Faust is coming from having seen a small but powerful moment of the effects of pure love. Does what he has just seen have an effect on him?

Faust is going to try to meet Marguerite again. He wants to exercise his *jeunesse*—to win her, possess her. But his desires are generalized, the desires of a man with little experience of life who has been brought suddenly out of old age and into youthfulness. They have arisen because he has seen how beautiful Marguerite is, and because Méphistophélès has promised her to him. They are not based on any knowledge of Marguerite—of any woman, really—nor of himself. He has had no experience to give him a foundation for his actions. Lacking Méphistophélès for the moment to push him along, he has to fall back on his own resources: he has to think about what he's facing.

So the aria is about discovering. It is not just a beautiful and challenging piece to sing; it is an essential part of the opera's action.

Before the aria proper, there is a three-line cavatina. It begins with a four-bar introduction, marked *andante* and *pianissimo* and presented as a moment of great calm. But is that perhaps the calm before the storm? In the third bar, there is a crescendo in the orchestra. Does this suggest uncertainty? Something is affecting Faust, and he does not know what it is; he asks: "Quel trouble inconnu me pénètre?" He is being overtaken with feelings he does not recognize. Why should he? After all, he has never looked outside his books before. In the second line there is a crescendo as Gounod helps him bring these feelings within reach of his understanding: "Je sens l'amour s'emparer de mon être." This culminates in a *forte* in the third line, specifically on the second word, "Marguerite!," which is packed full of the wonder Faust is feeling as he begins to understand the power of desire. But this not desire in only its carnal sense; what Faust is beginning to experience is love. This understanding is his *first discovery*. It is cued by the music, and it allows us to see the human being who is making the discovery, not just the hero with the big voice.

What happens in the aria? Lost in wonder, Faust romanticizes everything he sees: the dwelling is pure like the girl who lives there; poverty is rich; nature has protected Marguerite so that she could grow up to be a child of nature and, at the same time, a complete woman; she is an angel on earth. These are big thoughts. In fact, they are probably not thoughts at all—more like general impressions. But they have a strongly abstract quality, and abstractions cannot be acted. So the singer has to find specific and detailed actions to embody what he is learning. Faust sings his salutation, "Salut! demeure chaste et pure," twice. Is the first version somber? Casual? Formal?

Once a decision has been made, it leads to the repeat. In his first statement, Faust is trying to find the right words to describe the house, so he can hold back a little, searching; then, on the word "pure," he can realize he's found the right language—this is his *second discovery*—and then, on the repeat he can confirm the image he has discovered and move on to wondering at it and trying to understand it. There is a quarter rest before the second line; in that beat he fully realizes what it means that it is in this house that Marguerite lives: that is why the house is so pure, because she is "une âme innocente et divine."

Faust looks for images to describe his responses. He sees that Marguerite's cottage is poor. (This is important: in many productions I have seen, her cottage is presented as beautifully designed, picturesque. I have never forgotten the anecdote about the conductor Pierre Monteux, who, upon seeing an overly sumptuous set, exclaimed: "Marguerite est donc millionaire?") What Faust is looking at has to stimulate his imagination, and his imagination is teaching him that it is possible for a person's inner qualities to make his or her surroundings irrelevant. He says:

Que de richesse en cette pauvreté!   What richness in this poverty!
En ce réduit, que de félicité!   In this humble abode, what happiness!

If the cottage looks as if it has been designed for some kind of country life magazine, there is nothing for Faust's imagination to do (or the audience's, for that matter). What he sees leads him to a question: how can he explain the contradiction between what he thinks about Marguerite and the poverty of her living conditions? He can understand it only if he thinks about nature—or rather Nature, the creative agent of so many romantic sensibilities. This *third discovery* is a very big one for him, since when he was in his study reading books he would have contemptuously rejected any such idea. The next three lines show how startled Faust is, and we in the audience should be clear as to how new an idea this is for him:

Ô nature, c'est là que tu la fis   O Nature, it is here where you made her
  si belle!   beautiful!
C'est là que cette enfant a dormi sous ton   It is here where this child slept under
  aile,   your wing,
A grandi sous tes yeux!   Grew up before your eyes!

The lines are as much about him as they are about Marguerite. Once he has made this discovery, the rest of the aria can unfold as Faust relishes what he has learned:

Là que, que ton haleine enveloppant son âme,	Here, with your breath enveloping her soul,
Tu fis avec amour épanouir la femme	You lovingly made this woman
En cet ange des cieux!	Bloom into this angel of heaven!
C'est là! . . . oui . . . C'est là!	It is here . . . yes . . . here it is!

These are not discoveries; they are appreciations, or perhaps incantations—as is his repeat of the whole aria: he is going over in his mind what he has learned, almost as if he were memorizing a prayer. The religious term here is appropriate: the climax of the process is his further repetition of the aria's first two lines, with the brilliant high C on the second syllable of "presence." It is a mark of his recognition that Marguerite—her presence—is the incarnation of his love. Faust has come a long way from the person he was when he entered the scene with Méphistophélès, eager to satisfy his sexual appetite.

So when Méphistophélès returns, eager to move his pupil along to seduce Marguerite, Faust is overcome with shame; he wants to get away; he says, "Fuyons! Je veux ne jamais la revoir!" (Let's flee! I never want to see her again!). Why? He is about to get all he wanted; what's the problem? Well, he has seen her innocence and then idealized her so powerfully that it seems he cannot bear the thought of what he had earlier wanted, which was only to seduce her.

In any case, whatever his scruples, the action unfolds as it must. Méphistophélès leaves the casket of jewels on the threshold of Marguerite's cottage. She returns; she thinks of the young man she met at the fair (Faust); she sings her song "Il était un Roi de Thulé" (There was once a King of Thule); she sees the casket and opens it; she tries on the jewels, even though she knows she shouldn't; and she wishes the handsome young man were there to see her. With this the trap is sprung: she has given away her innocence, and nothing will be the same for her again. Méphistophélès' cruel joke, giving Faust not just what he asked for—youth—but rather giving him love, is unfolding.

The power of this cruelty is increased by what Faust has learned in this scene, what we in the audience must *see* him learn: that desire and love are not the same. What Faust learns, standing before Marguerite's cottage, is what makes him eager to go along with Méphistophélès' plot, while maybe thinking he is not. In reality he is just going after a pretty girl; in his imagination, though, she is more. It is this "more" that deepens the opera: it shows Faust gaining the capacity to think of someone outside himself, to be, to some extent, and for the moment, unselfish. It shows him learning to be something he had not asked to learn: not just to be young, but to be human.

He does not act on this right away; Méphistophélès' poison has sunk in too deeply. But it is this realization that, at the end of the opera, will make him demand that Méphistophélès bring him to Marguerite in prison, after she has murdered their child and been condemned to die. It is what makes him try to save her, even though it is he who is lost.

If we only experience the aria as a great song, a chance to emote, we will not see Faust learn what he learns, and the ending, which should be tragic, will be only sentimental, melodramatic, and thin.

The Da Capo Aria: Handel, *Xerxes*, Act I, Scenes 1–3, and Act III, Scene 11

I have said that no aria should end the way it began. Progress should occur—a discovery, a decision, perhaps a resolution—and should be evident to the audience. Progress should occur because action is happening, because a character is changing: getting closer to what he wants, avoiding trouble, or accepting what cannot be changed. Action works through conflict; characters act to overcome barriers, to move ahead. It is action that energizes the drama on the stage. The progress that should occur in an aria is part of the dramatic action of the whole opera.

The aria in baroque opera, typically the da capo aria, challenges this. In its most common form, the da capo aria has three parts: a statement, then a different statement (which may either contrast directly with the first one or show an entirely fresh attitude or point of view), and finally a repetition of the first statement, usually with vocal elaborations. But how can turning back help a character move forward? How can the da capo aria end differently than it began?

Broadly speaking, in baroque opera the recitatives carry the action and establish the conflicts. The arias are not driven by narrative or plot. They allow us to see the characters' highly personal response to the conflicts revealed in the recitative. Time freezes as we watch characters wrestling with the consequences and effects of those conflicts. We watch as characters verbalize their innermost, sometimes heartrending and painful truths. And because the revelation of those truths—the self-discovery—gives the characters an awareness of self that they did not have before, they end the aria very differently, with new information about themselves.

When they are finished, we return to the main action. So arias stand, to some extent, outside time and outside the opera's time of action. In a sense all arias do this, but the style of baroque opera seria takes the conventional aria to the extreme. Action in the recitatives, reaction in the arias, few ensembles or duets—where is the drama?

Until fairly recently Handel's operas, though praised for their music and recognized as classics of the baroque, have been thought to be dramatically inert. Here is a paragraph from Winton Dean, the Handel scholar who has been largely responsible for helping us see how the operas can come alive. He describes the old view:

> We used to be told—and sometimes still are—that *opera seria* was little more than a concert in costume. The singers, it was supposed, advanced in turn to address their arias to the audience without regard to anyone else who happened to be on stage. The recitatives, devoid of musical content, then altered the situation, preparing the way for another character's similarly restricted utterance. Since there were very few duets or ensembles, in some operas none at all apart from the usually perfunctory *coro* at the end, there was no opportunity for the characters to strike sparks off one another in the manner of later opera. The implication is that *opera seria* had no backbone or dramatic thrust, especially as the individual arias, nearly all in da capo form, were generally confined to the expression of a single emotion or *Affekt*. (Donald Burrows, ed., *The Cambridge Companion to Handel* [Cambridge, 1997], 249)

Against this Dean makes strong claims for the dramatic power of Handel's operas.

> One of Handel's most memorable and least understood achievements is the skill with which he integrated scenic and musical conventions to enlarge the dramatic scale. By a flexibility of tonality, by so placing the arias that they simultaneously advanced the plot and developed the characters, facet by facet, and by the variety and ingenuity of his treatment of da capo form, especially in the expansion, contraction, or omission of orchestral ritornellos, Handel ensured that the opera, far from falling into detached segments, was in continuous, fluid motion. The listener's interest is not only held but constantly drawn forward. (Ibid., 253)

My experience as both a director and an audience member leads me to the conclusion that Handel's operas can be powerfully dramatic when the singers are committed to the words and to the music, when the relationships between characters and their objectives are clear, and when the singing is very good.

We will look at three aspects of Handel's opera *Serse* (or, in the more familiar English version, *Xerxes*): how character is established and developed in the relationship between recitative and aria, how the drama grows as scene succeeds scene, and how progress occurs both in and by means of the da capo aria.

Xerxes was first produced in London on April 15, 1738. It played for only five performances and was not staged again for almost two hundred years. It was the last opera Handel wrote but one (*Semele*, in 1743) and the last one produced for a regular opera season, since he moved instead to the oratorio and the nonstaged musical dramas that he thought would please his English audiences more. *Xerxes* was based in turn on an adaptation, made in 1694, of Francesco Cavalli's opera *Xerses*, written in 1655 (Cavalli was a pupil of Monteverdi).

The subject of the opera is the misplaced love of the hero, the Persian king Xerxes, for one of his subjects, Romilda. Many plot twists and reversals occur before Xerxes is finally united with the woman he should marry (Amastre), and Romilda can marry the man she loves, Xerxes' brother, Arsamene. Xerxes is a historical figure. King of Persia from 485 to 465 BC, he who brought a great military force to invade the tiny Greek states and was defeated by them at several key battles (Thermopylae, Salamis, and Plataea). Although this is not the part of Xerxes' life that interests Handel, it is still visible behind the main plot, and we should know a little more about it in order to better understand where both the character and the composer are coming from. This kind of research is what both director and singers would undertake before a production. We know most about Xerxes from the Greek writer Herodotus, the author of *The History*, written in the mid-400s BC to describe the causes of the wars between the Greeks and the Persians and explain how a fractious group of small city-states could successfully defend themselves against one of the superpowers of the time. Part of his explanation was to contrast the way the two peoples were governed. He showed, for example, that all Persians were slaves of their king, utterly subject to his rule; by contrast, even though the Greek cities governed themselves in different ways, still, all Greeks were citizens. Herodotus's characterization of Xerxes is intended to show how an absolute ruler, a tyrant, behaves. To do this he tells stories, mostly based on anecdotes he has collected. For example, he tells how, on his way with his army to invade Greece, Xerxes commanded that a bridge be built across the Hellespont (the Dardanelles, a strait of water separating Asia and Europe, about two-thirds of a mile wide) so that his army could pass over it. A storm destroyed the bridge, so Xerxes ordered his men to lash the Hellespont three hundred times and to lower into the water a yoke of fetters; he then beheaded the bridge's engineers. (In Act II, scene 8 of *Xerxes*, a chorus of

Christopher Newcomer as Xerxes in a scene from a 2009 Maryland Opera Studio production of Handel's Xerxes. *(Photo by Cory Weaver)*

sailors praises Xerxes for having built the bridge; later, in scene 11, there is a reference to a mighty storm, but that is all Handel has to say about it.) Later, after he had the bridge rebuilt and successfully crossed into Europe, Xerxes was entertained by one of the richest of his subjects, a man who had given most of his fortune to support Xerxes' war and whose four younger sons were joining the army. In return, the man asked Xerxes if his oldest son could be left behind. This enraged Xerxes: he ordered the young man's body to be cut in half and had his army march between the two parts. What these stories show is Xerxes' extraordinary sense of his own rights, of what was due him; we see how far he was ready to go to protect these rights, his savagery if crossed, his absolute command over his people. The Xerxes of the opera is clearly not such a man, but these tyrannical and monstrous qualities lie behind Handel's character and should not be forgotten.

Who, then, is the character that Handel presents as the hero of his opera? We learn a lot about this from the first two scenes; we also learn a lot about how Handel creates character. After the overture, the first scene opens with Xerxes standing alone onstage, gazing at a plane tree. After a recitative, he sings a brief *arioso*, "Ombra mai fù" (an *arioso* has the melodic qualities, but not the form, of an aria; in other words, the da capo aria's ABA structure is lacking):

Frondi tenere, e belle del mio platano amato, per voi risplenda il Fato. Tuoni, lampi, e procelle non v'oltraggino mai la cara pace, nè giunga a profanarvi austro rapace. Ombra mai fù di vegetabile cara ed amabile soave più.	May Fate shine upon you, tender and beautiful leaves of my beloved plane tree. May thunder, lightning, and storm never outrage your precious peace, nor the rapacious south wind profane you. Never was nature's own shade more loved or sweetly treasured than yours.

It is a very striking scene, and the music is exquisitely beautiful. So beautiful, in fact, that it is often cut out of its context and presented as a concert piece. Dramatically, in the context for which it was intended, it makes us wonder—a man making some kind of love to a tree? What is going on? How is a singer to approach this seriously?

Handel gives Xerxes plenty of opportunity to examine the tree, to think about what it means to him. There is an introduction of fourteen bars. The tempo is marked *larghetto*, and the dynamics are *piano* for five bars, *forte* for two bars, *piano* again for two bars, and finally *forte* for five bars. These dynamic changes give the singer space that can be filled with specific actions as he (or she—the part, originally written for castrato, is now sung by either a male countertenor or a female mezzo-soprano) prepares to sing the *arioso*. The audience can take advantage of this space, too, filling it with their own questions. Who is this? What does he want? Why is he singing a love song to a tree?

The singer will work out his or her analysis in the usual way. Here is one set of possibilities. We do not know where Xerxes is coming from, since no direct information is given in the libretto; Xerxes simply appears and sings. We do know some things, however: we know that Xerxes is king of Persia, we can imagine what this might mean in terms of his cares and responsibility, and we know that he is alone. The singer, who knows what happens in the whole opera, knows (from Act II, scenes 8 and 11) that this incident happens as Xerxes is bringing his great army to invade the Greeks. So we can imagine that his life is full of stress from the responsibility of leading an invasion, or just from being the king. He is going into a garden, and his words imply that he's particularly struck by the simple and natural qualities of the tree and its beauty. That's his *first discovery*. He is also struck by its vulnerability and hopes that it can be preserved from a less tender nature, the nature of storms and tempests, which might damage it. That is his *second discovery*. He is also moved by the protection the tree gives him from the sun. That is his *third discovery*. It is as if this tree, in its simplicity and beauty, gives him something he cannot get anywhere else—calm, perhaps, and a sense of natural ease. Nature itself might prevent him from getting what he wants if, with its storms, it damages the tree. And his job—being king—might prevent him from finding contentment; perhaps the storms that could damage the tree resemble the storms of pressure that invade his daily life. In effect, he is praying that Fate, "il Fato," will protect the tree. And, by extension, him: it is not hard to imagine some form of projection in Xerxes' admiration of the tree's solitary and vulnerable beauty.

This image is not unusual for its time; in fact, it is a pretty familiar picture—a man seeking pastoral ease, a moment's freedom from the pressures and demands of state. It is not passive; it is full of action, the actions of seeking and desiring. The first two discoveries Xerxes makes occur in the recitative, the third in the *arioso*. There are plenty of actions a singer can choose to show Xerxes making these discoveries. But none of the discoveries changes his overall objective, which is to think about the plane tree and say what his attitude is toward it. (Of course, if the singer thinks the scene is ridiculous and lets this show, or even just tries to sing beautifully without any sense of why the aria has to be sung, then the whole dynamic of the scene is lost.) We can infer from the singer's actions that there is some kind of emptiness in Xerxes' life; after all, if the only peace he can find is with a tree, he must be pretty completely alone. That is what we in the audience discover.

What happens next, in the two scenes that follow, gives a context for this that leads us to understand better who Xerxes is, where he is coming from, what he wants, and what may block him. The drama is being created as we move from scene to scene.

Arsamene, Xerxes' brother, appears with his servant, Elviro. It might look at first as if these two have stepped out of another world, or another opera.

ARSAMENE
Siam giunti, Elviro . . .

ARSAMENE
We have arrived, Elviro . . .

ELVIRO
Intendo.

ELVIRO
I understand.

ARSAMENE
Dove alberga . . .

ARSAMENE
Where is the house . . .

ELVIRO
Seguite!

ELVIRO
I follow.

ARSAMENE
L'idol mio.

ARSAMENE
of my idol.

ELVIRO
Dite pure.

ELVIRO
Really.

ARSAMENE
Oh, se fortuna . . .

ARSAMENE
Oh, if Fortune . . .

ELVIRO
Sì; così è . . .

ELVIRO
I think so; absolutely . . .

ARSAMENE
Tu, dove vai?

ARSAMENE
Where are you going?

ELVIRO
Men vado ad appoggiarmi che
   di sonno io cado.

ELVIRO
To lean up against that tree
   before I fall asleep.

ARSAMENE
Vien qui pronto ti dico.

ARSAMENE
Come back here right now.

The comic servant is conventional: his focus is on basic needs—here, how to get some rest—puts the higher aspirations of his master into a quasi-comic context. What his master wants is to get close to where he thinks Romilda will be, since he is in love with her (as, we soon learn, she is with him). Like his brother, Arsamene is a seeker, only he knows what he wants and is seeking an actual person; Xerxes knows what he lacks, but not yet what he wants. So, by the end of scene 2 we have three characters in search of something—the king wants something to fill the void in his life, his brother wants Romilda, and Elviro wants to rest his weary bones. The potential is there for conflict between Xerxes and Arsamene. Having Elviro present reminds us that this is a comedy, not a tragedy, and suggests that, however grand the needs or aspirations of his betters may be, however tragic they may seem from time to time, a way will always be found for life to go on. The scene ends with Romilda's appearance.

First we hear her music, then she begins her recitative; it is interrupted by exclamations from both Arsamene and Elviro; Xerxes enters just in time (at the beginning of scene 3) to hear the end of the recitative; finally she sings her *arioso*.

ROMILDA
O voi, che penate per
cruda beltà!
Un Xerxes ...

ROMILDA
Oh you who suffer at the hands of
cruel beauty:
Behold Xerxes ...

XERXES
Qui si canta il mio nome?

XERXES
Do I hear my name being sung?

ROMILDA
Un Xerxes mirate, che d'un ruvido
tronco acceso stà, e pur non
corrisponde altro al
suo amor, che mormorio di fronde!

ROMILDA
Behold Xerxes, aglow with
passion for nothing more than a
coarse tree-trunk, his love answered
only by the murmur of leaves!

Romilda is standing on a belvedere, which is how she has been able to overhear Xerxes. Apart from that, all we know about her is that Arsamene is in love with her. She is a figure of desire, not a historical personage; thus, we will learn about her only as the action unfolds. We can imagine, though, since we know why Arsamene has come to her house, that she is waiting for him. She has come outside hoping to see Arsamene; she wants to greet her beloved. But Arsamene is not there; instead, she hears Xerxes singing of his love for the plane tree. Having overheard his song, she thinks about what she has just heard. She thinks of Xerxes, who is full of need but has no one to love; she too is alone, since she does not know that Arsamene is there;

unlike Xerxes, who thinks only of his own state, her mind moves outward, imagining others. Like Xerxes, she sings to someone (or something, in his case). The verb "penate" is plural, so she has a specific group in mind—as she says, people who are suffering from love.

Her music is reflective, elegiac, as was Xerxes'. Are her comments about Xerxes mocking or sympathetic? Why not both? The mockery, if it is there, is not harsh; it is softened by the sympathy evident in the music. This gives us an image of Romilda as sympathetic and thoughtful; perhaps that is why she is so easy for the men in the opera to love. And it helps us see Xerxes a little differently, from the outside, as isolated and desolate: "e pur non corrisponde altro al suo amor, che mormorio di fronde." This adds understanding to what has been added already. It gives a richer context, a better understanding of Xerxes: he appears more complex, perhaps even more human. It also gives us a pretty good idea of what is going to happen next: here is Xerxes, full of desire and loneliness; there is Romilda, full of desirability. And all the while Elviro remains leaning up against the tree, simply because he is tired. Unfortunately, Arsamene, whom Romilda already loves, is in the way of what Xerxes discovers (when he sees her) he wants; it is this conflict that sets the action of the opera going.

So we are presented at the beginning of the opera with characters we know nothing about, characters about whom we have to learn as the scenes open out and play off each other. Progress—in the action, in our understanding—occurs through, and by means of, the movement from recitative to *arioso* and the movement from scene to scene. We in the audience have questions and make discoveries as we watch the action unfold. To see Xerxes alone (with the plane tree) is to immediately wonder why he is alone, where he is going, and what he wants. Handel's dramatic instincts are strong. The actions the singer finds to show what could be going on in Xerxes' mind will lead us to begin to answer these questions, so that progress occurs and the opera's action is under way.

Now for the da capo. Does progress occur? *Can* it occur?

Almost at the end of the opera, Xerxes has a spectacular aria, full of wild rage, that shows him pushed almost beyond his limit. Of course, his behavior has always been spectacular; from his first appearance in front of the plane tree through all his schemes to win Romilda and thwart his brother, we have seen that he can think only about himself and about getting his own way, no matter whom he may hurt to do so. So for him to be distressed here because his will is being thwarted seems only just. The aria seems to sum up all that is most ungoverned and violent in his character.

But before we can see what is going on in the aria, we have to step back and look at what leads up to it. Here is a list of the main characters, especially the ones who are involved in the opera's last scenes, some of whom we've met already:

- Xerxes, King of Persia
- Arsamene, Xerxes' half-brother
- Romilda, daughter of Ariodate, who loves Arsamene but who is pursued by Xerxes
- Ariodate, Romilda's father, Xerxes' vassal and the commander of his army
- Amastre, heiress of a neighboring kingdom and betrothed to Xerxes
- Atalanta, sister of Romilda, who plots to win Arsamene away from her sister

Act III, scene 11 is crowded with incident. The recitative, an encounter between Xerxes and Arsamene that takes up most of the scene, is crucial to Xerxes' aria, since it provides the discoveries and reversals that make the aria necessary. Here is the complete scene.

XERXES
Sene viene Ariodate. È tempo
omai di scoprir, che son io, che
Romilda desìo. Eccomi, Ariodate!

XERXES
Here comes Ariodates. The time
has come to reveal to him that I
want Romilda. Here I am, Ariodates!

ARIODATE
Invitto Sire, v'inchino . . .

ARIODATE
Oh, invincible lord, I bow before you . . .

XERXES
Or che vi sembra?
Lo sposo egual vi dissi . . .

XERXES
What do you say to this?
The groom I had told you about . . .

ARIODATE
È un alto onore!

ARIODATE
The honour is great!

XERXES
Romilda vaga ne sarà paga?

XERXES
Will fair Romilda be happy with it?

ARIODATE
Non brama più.

ARIODATE
She yearns for nothing more.

XERXES
Ma perchè non viene?
Dov'è?

XERXES
But why does she not come?
Where is she?

ARIODATE
Collo sposo.

XERXES
Come?

ARIODATE
Collo sposo, Signor.

XERXES
Che sposo? Ahimè!

ARIODATE
Come imponeste.

XERXES
Che imposi? Che?

ARIODATE
Eguale a voi, del vostro sangue,
è venne nelle mie
stanze ...

XERXES
E sono sposi?

ARIODATE
Sono.

XERXES
Empio! Perfido!
Indegno!

ARIODATE
Mio Rè ...

XERXES
Tu m'hai tradito! E pur, "tuo Re"
tenti chiamarmi, ardito!
*(Un piaggio porta una lettera a
Xerxes, egli parla basso.)*
Romilda a me l'invia? Perfida
donna!
Crede co' inchiostri rei
incantar follemente i sdegni miei?

ARIODATE
(Perchè non moro, o Ciel!)

ARIODATE
With the husband.

XERXES
What?

ARIODATE
With her husband, my lord.

XERXES
What husband?—Ah!

ARIODATE
The one you decreed.

XERXES
Decreed by me? What?

ARIODATE
Of your standing and of your own kin—
he came but a short while ago to my
residence ...

XERXES
And are they married?

ARIODATE
They are.

XERXES
Oh the treacherous, perfidious,
unworthy!

ARIODATE
My king ...

XERXES
You have betrayed me! And still you
have the audacity to call me your king!
*(A page brings him a letter.
Aside.)*
From Romilda? Oh, the perfidious
woman!
She believes she can calm
my outrage with the charms of her pen!

ARIODATE
(Why do I not die, oh heavens!)

XERXES
Leggi!
(da la lettera ad Ariodate, che
legge)
Che fai?

XERXES
Read this out!
(Hands the letter to Ariodates, who
reads it.)
Well?

ARIODATE
"Ingratissimo amante!"

ARIODATE
"Oh most thankless lover,"

XERXES
Come! Ingrato mi chiama? E
tanto ella osa?

XERXES
What! Does she call me thankless?
How dare she?

ARIODATE
"Venni per esser vostra."

ARIODATE
"I came here to be yours."

XERXES
E altrui si sposa?

XERXES
And she marries someone else?

ARIODATE
"Trovai che mi sprezzate."

ARIODATE
"And found that you have scorned me."

XERXES
Oh, note scellerate!

XERXES
Oh, villainous letter!

ARIODATE
"Parto; ma il Ciel punirà
vostra colpe."

ARIODATE
"I am leaving; but the heavens will
punish your offense."

XERXES
Colpe d'averti amato!

XERXES
The offense of having loved you!

ARIODATE
"Io piangerò sin all'ultimo fiato.
Amastre."

ARIODATE
"I shall weep till my death.
Amastre."

XERXES
Che?

XERXES
What?

ARIODATE
Non di Romilda è il foglio.

ARIODATE
This note was not written by Romilda.

XERXES
(prende con sdegno la lettera e guarda
la ferma)
Amastre! Vanne, e ti allontana,
indegno! Non mancava altro
tedio in tanto sdegno!

XERXES
(incensed, he grabs the letter and looks
at the signature)
Amastre! Get out, you unworthy one!
This is not the provocation
I need in the face of such ridicule!

The singer's analysis of how Xerxes can enter this scene might go like this. Earlier, in scene 5, he had made his plans for marrying Romilda by getting her father to arrange for her to marry "sposo del nostro sangue" (a man of my blood), though he did not tell Ariodate exactly who that man would be. (Why not? Why was Xerxes coy with his own vassal? Did he want to hold back the pleasure of seeing Ariodate's face when he realizes it is he, the king, who is going to marry his daughter? Or is it his assumption that he is the only one of the "blood"?) As far as he was concerned, he had dealt with what he found out in scene 7 (that Romilda and Arsamene were lovers) and sentenced his brother to death. So the obstacle to his getting everything he wants has been, he thinks, removed. He is going to meet Ariodate and Romilda. He wants to reveal to Ariodate that it is he, Xerxes, who will be marrying Romilda so he can take possession of her. Romilda is not present, so he asks Ariodate, who is just coming in, where Romilda is. This is a high point for Xerxes. It seems to him that he has gotten everything he wanted; all that is left is for him to enjoy his new possession.

Ariodate is coming into the scene from having carried out, as he thinks, the king's instructions, so he is thinking with pleasure about what this will mean for him. He is going to report to his master. He wants to tell Xerxes that he has done what he was told to do and bask in the glory of being the king's father-in-law. The only possible obstacle would be change of mind on Xerxes' part. Since Ariodate lives to obey, he would have to find a way to please his king. Like Xerxes, Ariodate is at a high point; he too has everything he could have wanted, if not more: through his daughter, he is now part of the royal family. So, like Xerxes, he enters the scene full of expectations.

The recitative is structured by *reversals* as the expectations of each character are systematically thwarted by what he or she discovers. Handel develops the action toward each discovery with great precision. Xerxes' opening speech is full of delight and anticipation. He wants to reveal to Ariodate that it is he, the king, who will marry Romilda: "È tempo omai di scoprir, che son io, che Romilda desio" (this is an aside). He is like a little boy bursting with eagerness; he says, "Eccomi, Ariodate!" Ariodate is also excited: "Invitto Sire, v'inchino." Each can hardly contain himself; each is following out the logic of the situation as he understands it to be. And so Xerxes asks where Romilda is; logically, he wants to see her. And just as logically, Ariodate tells him that she is "collo sposo." And with that, the logic cracks: "Che sposo? Ahimè!" says Xerxes. Ariodate explains, "Come imponeste." Xerxes seems to be puzzled: "Che imposi? Che?" So Ariodate, nervously, tries to justify himself by giving the king's own words back to him: "Eguale a voi, del vostro sangue." But it does not work. Xerxes asks, though by now he knows the answer: "E sono sposi?" Ariodate answers that they are. At this, Xerxes explodes: "Empio! Perfido! Indegno!"

We in the audience already know the answer to Xerxes' question; we saw Romilda and Arsamene join their hands in marriage at the end of the previous scene. The question for us as we watch the opera is not "What happens next?" but "How will people react?" Because our attention is on the characters' reactions, the actions the singers will choose must be as precise and clear as is the text. We should be able to see Xerxes' transitions from gleeful expectancy, to uncertainty, to disbelief, to rage and despair. Handel's words give singers these transitions; his recitatives move, they have the rhythms and tempi of natural speech. The accompaniment should support and foster this; the continuo players and the singers must work closely together to achieve these rhythms and tempi.

Xerxes' objective on entering the scene was clear: to enjoy telling Ariodate that it is he, Xerxes, who will be marrying Romilda, then to enjoy taking possession of his bride. Having discovered that Romilda is already married to Arsamene, he has a new intention, to blame Ariodate: "Tu m'hai tradito!" Immediately there is another challenge: the letter that he thinks may be from Romilda but then discovers is from Amastre. What is his new intention? As we know, all his choices have been taken away from him, leaving him powerless and humiliated, in a kind of vacuum. So pretty much all he can do at this point is explode. His objective, in his aria, is to express himself, to release his frustrations.

Xerxes' final lines in the recitative before his aria show him moving toward this and thus give his reasons for singing it:

XERXES	XERXES
(prende con sdegno la lettera e guarda la ferma)	*(incensed, he grabs the letter and looks at the signature)*
A mastre! Vanne, e ti allontana, indegno! Non mancava altro tedio in tanto sdegno!	Amastre! Get out, you unworthy one! This is not the provocation I need in the face of such disdain!

These are tricky lines. There are many choices for the singer: relief that the cruel letter was not from Romilda, anger that his plans have fallen apart and he has lost Romilda to his brother, embarrassment that the woman to whom he has been betrothed has caught him trying to seduce another woman. An eight-bar introduction gives the singer the chance to explore different possibilities and to find actions for them. It also suggests what his state of mind is: the sixteenth notes in the bass and descending 32nd-note scales spanning more than an octave reveal that his anger is not cold and calculated; it is wild, the passion of a cornered animal.

The aria's challenges are great. It is a very "big" sing, with some extremely florid passages and a higher tessitura than any of Xerxes' previous arias. Also, it comes almost at the end of the opera, when the singer playing Xerxes has already sung two and a half acts, so great stamina is required. And then there's the typical da capo aria structure, the ABA form, which poses its own problems. Here's the aria:

Crude furie degl' orridi abissi,	Oh savage Furies from the hideous abysses,
Aspergetemi d'atro veleno!	Smother me with your poison!
Crolli il mondo, e'l sole s'eclissi	May the world cave in and the sun be eclipsed by my fury,
A quest'ira, che spira il mio seno!	And may my breast finally meet its end!

To whom is Xerxes singing the aria? Ariodate has withdrawn to one side of the stage, so for all intents and purposes he is not there, and the other characters—Arsamene, Romilda, Amastre, Atalanta, and Elviro—appear only after his aria, as Xerxes is leaving. Why is this an important question for the singer? Simply because it gives a point of focus and helps the singer be clear about the aria's purpose. If his purpose is to express his rage and frustration, the form it takes is that of a prayer—not unlike the Countess's "Porgi amor" in *Le nozze di Figaro*—only here it is the Furies to whom Xerxes is praying, not to the god of love.

What Xerxes says he wants in this aria is to die: "che spiro il mio seno!" So his objective is to get the Furies to kill him. But not only him: like Lear on the heath, he wants the whole universe to come to an end: "Crolli il mondo." He expresses this by means of great intensity, highly dramatic and florid singing, and many, many repetitions. Which brings us to the point: how can the aria be sung so that it is not just a vocal tour de force? How can the singer find the drama in the aria?

If we wrote out the words, as sung, to show all the repetitions in the first A section, they would read:

Crude furie degli' orridi abissi, aspergetemi, aspergetemi, aspergetemi d'atro veleno! Aspergetemi crude furie, crude furie degli' orridi abissi, aspergetemi d'atro veleno, d'atro veleno! Crude furie degli' orridi abissi, crude furie degl' orridi abissi, aspergetemi d'atro veleno, aspergetemi d'atro veleno, d'atro veleno, aspergetemi, crude furie, crude furie, degl' orridi abissi, aspergetimi d'atro veleno!

That is a lot of repetition. How to find the drama? One singer I worked with, who wanted to find effective dramatic choices and actions that would show these choices, assigned verbs to certain phrases, verbs such as "attacking," "plotting," "defying," "demanding," and pleading." (*The importance of verbs cannot be overstated—they denote action and are the only kind of word that can be acted.*) Thus each phrase was given a mini-objective within the larger, overall objective. Experimenting in rehearsal with this series of mini-objectives and the transitions between them helped give dramatic shape to the A section and at the same time prepared for the transition to the B section. Whereas the A is fully *vivace*, the B is different: it begins with great force, straightforwardly, and then becomes almost calm, perhaps resigned. The music is not as violent or as complicated as in the A sections. Rage gives way to a more considered desire for revenge. After the first words of the B section ("Crolli il mondo") the thought stops, to be replaced by an outburst of pure rage, as a series of sixteenth notes is heard in the orchestra. Then Xerxes says "e'l sole s'eclissi," and again the orchestra interrupts his thoughts in another series of sixteenth notes. Finally Xerxes completes his thought: "à quest'ira, che spira il mio seno," and this is repeated with a melismatic line that reflects his state. The B section tempo marking is *adagio*. In going beyond the personal here and universalizing his anger, Xerxes seems to reach some kind of temporary conclusion: imagining the world ending leads him to think again of himself and ask for his own end. This change makes sense in purely human terms, since it is impossible to maintain a high level of pure rage for very long. But the change is temporary; seeing the possibility of his own death throws him back to the A section and its furious intensity, and so he renews his prayer: "Crude furie!" There is a practical benefit to the singer if he can make these transitions: it lets him be very still in reaching the end of the B section, with its strong sense of finality, and this in turn prepares him for yet another assault on the fioritura heights of the A. But it also shows Xerxes himself changing. The way he sings the A section the second time, after having sung the B, must be different because of something he has realized in the B. What might that be? I do not think his overall objective has changed: he still wants to be drenched in the "veleno" of the Furies. But perhaps his intention is different. Perhaps he goes from intense personal rage in the A, to a desire for the entire world to end as well as a focus on himself and his own end (both in the B), and then, in the second statement of the A, back to the same words as in the beginning but with a greater sense of disgust at his own life and circumstances. What happens in the first part of the final scene shows him still caught up in his angry behavior. But we do have a sense that, having experienced the extremes of his feelings, he is now ready for anything—including the mighty change that will come in the final scene, when he is able finally to accept the reality that is before him, ask for forgiveness, and wish everyone well:

Amici, compatite i miei furori e godete felici i vostri amori!	Forgive my past ill humour, good friends, and be happy in your love!

We may choose to believe in this benevolence or not. But, for Handel, the plot is resolved, the curtain is down, and the revelers can return to ordinary life.

So progress does occur, and the da capo aria ends differently from the way it began. The reason it does is that the singer has paid attention to the words as well as the music, has taken advantage of the dramatic opportunities both provide, has made sure that he or she understands how the aria both comes out of the recitatives and returns to them, has found actions that let him or her show clearly the objectives of his character, and has sung his or her character with full dramatic commitment.

6

Playing the Forms: Comedy and Tragedy

I S THERE A SPECIAL WAY to play comedy or tragedy? Are there tricks singers can use make sure they get their laughs or, conversely, make the audience weep?

The answer is: no. Singers should not try to be funny or work at being sad. Humor and sadness will emerge from the action; they must not be imposed on it. Here is a very pure, even quintessential, example of a comedy, taken from outside the world of opera. I think it makes the point.

Playing the Story, Not the Form

What is it that makes people laugh?

Often performers are not sure they know how to be funny. Many young performers, and even many experienced ones, think that the way to *be* funny is to *do* something funny, to act absurdly in order to show absurdity. This, they think, will get them their laugh. Nothing could be further from the truth. Timing, word emphasis, and rhythms are the tools that make comedy succeed.

The place to start—in a comedy, as in any other dramatic form—is always with the action. If a character's actions can be found, along with how they fit with the actions of the others in a scene, the character will have a good grasp of the scene's overall logic. If that logic is absurd, simply following the actions out will let the absurdity emerge on its own, unforced. Then all the singer has to do is perform the actions required in the scene. As likely as not, the laughs will follow. Comedy comes from the actions of characters following out the logic of their situations, not from tricks or mugging.

Abbott and Costello's "Who's on first?" sketch shows this very clearly. It is a classic, because from beginning to end it never deviates from the logic of its premise: that the names of the baseball players Abbott is trying to tell Costello about are unusual—"peculiar," as he says. Their peculiarities make perfect sense to him. But Costello, even though he uses most of the normal resources of language in trying to understand what Abbott is saying, simply cannot grasp them. Nor can Abbott, for his part, understand why Costello cannot understand what he, as simply and directly as he can, is saying.

The set-up is that Costello is going to New York to play baseball and Abbott has been given a coaching job on the same team. (In itself, this is a good joke: short, tubby Costello playing professional ball?) Costello is naturally curious and wants to know the names of the other players; that is his objective. Abbott wants to tell him; that is his objective.

> *Abbott*: Oh, I'll tell you their names, but you know it seems to me they give these ball players nowadays very peculiar names.
> *Costello*: You mean funny names?
> *Abbott*: Strange names, pet names . . . Like Dizzy Dean . . .

From here it is a short step to the beginning of the action of the joke:

> *Abbott*: Well, let's see, we have on the bags, Who's on first, What's on second, I Don't Know is on third . . . .

To Abbott this makes perfect sense. All he is doing is telling what he knows; he is giving Costello the players' names. That they are "peculiar" he has already made clear. To Costello, what Abbott has just said makes a different kind of sense, equally logical. He hears Abbott say, "Who," "What," and "I Don't Know," but since he cannot hear the capital letters, he has no way of knowing that Abbott is naming people; instead he thinks that Abbott is saying he does not know the players' names. So he says, "That's what I want to find out." Each is, from his own perspective, perfectly logical and quite correct. But we in the audience, who can understand both sides, can see how far apart they are. And the comedy of the piece arises from this gap.

What makes it work so well is that the logic of the situation never lapses. If, at any point, Costello had said to Abbott something like, "Oh, I get it. The players' nicknames are really parts of speech or sentences," the absurdity would have vanished, replaced by common sense. But then it would not be funny anymore.

In the piece, neither character changes. Each has a point of view and an objective; each behaves in a certain way because of what he believes to be true. There is no need at any point for mugging. What each must show in his voice is what the logic of his position requires—growing frustration. Anything else would get in the way. There are no discoveries in the sketch that might take either character out of his trap, and therefore the objectives never change; they simply collide.

Comedy might in fact be described as a drama of collisions. Usually a collision in comedy involves at least one character who is obsessive or rigid, who wants something or believes something so intensely that he is unable to learn or adapt to the reality that is before him. Often these rigid characters are identifiable members of a particular social class—an arrogant aristocrat, a miserly merchant—and they collide with characters who are adaptable—a tricky servant, a scheming lover. In this case the action of the comedy might be to expose not just the weakness of a rigid individual, but the absurdities and limitations of his social order. Depending on the emphasis given to the criticism, this kind of comedy can tend toward satire. Or the rigid character—an old man who wants a young wife, say—collides with a young woman who also wants to get married, but not to him. In this case he is a blocking figure who gets in the way of what could be called a life force. This is romantic comedy, as old as the Greek dramatist Menander, and it is resolved when the young woman and her chosen lover are able to get around the blocks and come together. In both cases, the action of the comedy moves toward some new grouping of characters at the end, usually composed of those who can be more adaptable, sometimes dramatized in the form of a dinner. In both cases, the rigid or blocking character may or may not be invited to join the "new society," to come to dinner. If he is kept out, then the comedy can have a tragic overtone. If he is let in, it is because he is able to show he can change, just enough, and the tone can be fully celebratory.

Collisions in comedies usually involve surprise and reversal. This is as true for a single moment of comedy as it is for the actions of larger scenes. The encounter between the shoe of a pompous, well-dressed man and a banana peel takes only a second, but the reversal he experiences as his posterior comes into contact with the pavement is completely surprising for him, and probably for us in the audience as well. It is not even necessary for us to be surprised: a director could make us see the banana peel as the man moves toward it, then—bingo!—our expectations would be rewarded. (Or the surprise is that the man has, unknown to us in the audience, seen the banana and steps over it.) The surprise Falstaff faces in the last act of Verdi's opera as he is exposed, cowering, at the foot of Herne's Oak and wearing horns (a version of the horns he had hoped to apply to Ford) takes longer to establish, but its effects on him are no less powerful and no less a reversal of his expectations. We in the audience might be surprised by how Falstaff reacts, in his surprise, but not by what surprises him, since we have all along been in the know.

Often, as these examples show, there is an element of detachment for the audience in comedy. When we laugh at either Falstaff or the pompous man, we are not thinking primarily of the hurt each is experiencing, to either body or vanity. What we laugh at is the surprising reversal. Both the well-dressed man and Falstaff had seemed so sure of themselves, so set in their intentions, so unaware of possible dangers. Now, in an instant, each is reduced, dropped far below the level of his aspirations into ordinariness. Since the ordinary is the region most of us in the audience inhabit, we can be secretly pleased to see their pride (literally, in the case of the pompous man) going before a fall, to see their vanity punished by humiliation. If we are left in that position, of enjoying the reversals suffered by others, then the comedy can be pretty black—again, tending toward satire.

But often it does not, moving instead toward some form of genial integration or celebration. That is why so often comedies end with scenes that are both conclusions of what has gone before and the promises of new things to come—recognitions, marriages, feasts. Even Falstaff is invited to dinner at the end. And "Who's on first?," which ends in the same mutual incomprehension it began with, still encourages feelings of geniality: we know that Abbott and Costello will emerge from it, their performing personas intact, to perform other sketches and engender their own kinds of new futures. Which they, like all successful comedians, will do by following out the logic of their situations, by being true to the action of their piece.

Comedy: Donizetti, *Don Pasquale*, Act II, Scenes 2–5

A buffo is a comic actor, usually male and usually, in opera, a bass. The basso buffo plays the role of the gull, the person who is easily fooled or cheated. Usually he is a comedy's older man and starts out as the blocking figure, the character who gets in the way of true love and, for a while, prevents the handsome young hero from coming together with the beautiful young heroine. In a comedy such as *Falstaff* he is Falstaff himself; in *Le nozze di Figaro* and *Il barbiere di Seviglia* he is Bartolo; in Rossini's *L'italiana in Algeri* he is Mustafà; and in *Don Pasquale*, of course, he is Pasquale. *Don Pasquale* is called a *dramma buffa in tre atti*.

Why is the buffo so easily fooled? Because he has an obsession, and that prevents him from dealing adequately with reality. Falstaff is unable to deal with the possibility that his appetites cannot be satisfied, Bartolo (in Mozart's *Le nozze*) cannot bear not to take revenge or (in Rossini's *Il barbiere*) imagine not getting his hands on his ward and her inheritance, and Pasquale cannot imagine himself as anything other than a desirable husband for a young wife. They are puffed up, bloated with an inappropriate sense of their own desirability or importance. Puffed up? The etymology of buffo shows this: in English we have buffoon, in Italian *buffone*, in French *bouffon*, and in medieval Latin *bufo*, toad. Think of how the toad swells up to make himself larger when he is threatened. Just so, the buffo character is caught up in his own defensive strategy: the obsession can be a defense against some kind of vulnerability—aging, lost love, defeat. But because the obsessed don't deal well with reality, their obsessions tend to make them all the more vulnerable: they are what we might call unsuccessful coping mechanisms.

Donizetti composed *Don Pasquale* in just three months, beginning in October 1842; it was first performed at the Théâtre Italien in Paris on January 3, 1843. His librettist was Giovanni Ruffini, a relatively inexperienced writer, who based the story on a novel by Stefano Pavesi, *Ser Marcantonio*, at Donizetti's request. In fact, Donizetti rewrote so much of Ruffino's text that the librettist refused to put his name on the libretto. Clearly Donizetti knew what he wanted, and in fact *Don Pasquale* has remained one of his best-known and most often performed operas.

One of the director's jobs is to make the story clear, and one of the chief ways he or she does this is by making sure the characters can be fully realized onstage. To do this, the director has to know who the characters are. There are four major players in *Don Pasquale*: Don Pasquale, an elderly, wealthy gentleman; his nephew and perhaps heir, Ernesto; his doctor and friend, Malatesta; and Norina, the woman Ernesto loves. Of these, Norina is the one the libretto tells us least about. We are told several times of her poverty: Ernesto calls her "una giovine povera, ma onorata e virtuosa" (a young lady, but respectable and virtuous). But we are given nothing else, and that raises questions that directors and singers have to answer. Where does she come from? How might Ernesto and Malatesta have met her? How do we know she really is virtuous—she says she is, and so does Ernesto, but might Ernesto, even Malatesta, be deluding themselves? So, in preparing a production these questions have to be answered, to give Norina enough backstory to make her credible and to give the singer something to work with in presenting her character.

One way was to think of her as an actress. The theater is, after all, a place where pay is poor, where young men fall in love with actresses, and

Kevin Glavin as Pasquale, right, in a scene from a 1996 Glimmerglass Opera Festival production of Donizetti's Don Pasquale. *(Photo by George Mott)*

where doctors (without beepers) can go to escape leeches and patients. It is a perfect place for both Ernesto and Malatesta to meet Norina; at the same time, it is not a place where Pasquale is likely to go. Moreover, it suits the character of Norina as Donizetti reveals it to us. In the scenes where we see her for the first time (Act I, scene 4 and Act I, scene 5),[1] she shows herself as adept at performance, both in what she tells us when she is alone and in what she shows when Malatesta is there. Finally, in her scene with Pasquale (Act II, scene 3) all her dramatic talents are in evidence as, under Malatesta's direction, she convinces Pasquale that she is innocent and virtuous enough (as well as beautiful) to get him to marry her on the spot. So it made sense for Norina to be an actress. And that decision gave us an idea about the opera's setting.

Unusually, for the times, Donizetti set his opera contemporarily, in the 1840s. But after that first production, in January, 1843, it became fashionable to set the opera earlier, in the mid-eighteenth century. We (the designers and I) decided to go a little further back, to the mid-seventeenth century, when the theater was flourishing in Paris. It was a time when Molière's Théâtre du Palais Royal and the Théâtre Comédie Italienne were both active, the latter playing almost exclusively works in the *commedia dell'arte* tradition, influences of which can be seen in Donizetti's opera. Scripted plays, improvisational theater, and combinations of the two were popular. With its vigorous characters and its spirited music, *Don Pasquale* perfectly suits that time. And that let us make Norina, as an actress, part of that world, as well as allowing Ernesto and Malatesta opportunities to meet her.

The action of *Don Pasquale* has a clear, straightforward logic. An aging gentleman, Don Pasquale, has two preoccupations: to impose his will on his nephew, Ernesto, by making him marry the woman he has chosen for him (rather than Norina, the woman Ernesto loves), and to impose his will on time, so to speak, by himself marrying a young wife. Both preoccupations are signs of an obsession: the wish to be young again, a player with full powers on life's stage. The action of the piece is concerned with curing this obsession. It does this through a series of plots and disguises: first, by seeming to indulge the old man and get him married to an attractive and innocent young woman (played by the disguised Norina); then, by letting him see the consequence of getting what he wants—not the loving and biddable wife, eager to produce half-a-dozen "bamboli," but a strong-willed woman who wants only to spend his money and take a young lover. The point is to

---

1. The scene numbers are based on the Ricordi edition.

make Pasquale so unhappy that he renounces his foolish marriage. At the same time the plotters have to manage things so that Ernesto can marry Norina, but Norina as she really is, not as she has been pretending to be. Once the plots have succeeded and Pasquale has learned to act his age, the opera's logic is fulfilled and life can go on as it should, with the young in one another's arms and the old dispensing cash.

The opera's actions, its plots and strategies, are aimed to deceive. Two of the four principal characters are fooled at some point by the machinations of others. Pasquale is the one who is least aware of what is going on around him, and the greatest victim of others' plotting; this makes him the primary object of the comedy. Interestingly, Ernesto is himself out of the scheming until the opera is halfway done; once he understands what is happening, though, he participates fully in the plot. Norina needs to be filled in at times, but not often; none of the opera's comedy works at her expense. Only Dr. Malatesta, who seems to have no amorous or financial interests of his own, is never fooled. He is the chief plotter, and although he has to deal with the unexpected from time to time, his quick wits are always equal to the challenge. The audience, like Malatesta, generally knows what is going on. There are a few surprises for them, and some suspense over what might happen, but mostly they observe the actions that take place in the opera's world. The opera's conclusion, in which Norina takes the time to point a moral, only confirms what they've been thinking from the beginning:

La morale in tutto questo	The moral in all this
È assai facil di trovarsi:	Is very easy to find, in itself:
Ve la dico presto presto	I'll tell it to you right now
Se vi piace d'ascoltar.	If you'd like to hear it.
Ben è scemo di cervello	He's foolish in the head
Chi s'ammoglia in vecchia età, sì;	Who takes a wife in old age;
Va a cercar col campanello	It's like ringing a bell
Noie e doglie in quantità.	For troubles and pain in abundance.

Common sense with a bit of plotter's luck is what it takes to restore this world to balance, letting the old be old and the young get on with their lives. The challenge is to follow out the clear logic of the piece and find the comedy that is there, not to muddy the action with extraneous business.

Following the logic of the world in which comedy exists is of the utmost importance. Analysis of three scenes can show why: Pasquale's entrance with a servant, ready to meet "Sofronia"; the presentation of "Sofronia," involving Pasquale, Malatesta, and Norina, where two of the characters have double roles to play; and finally the entrance of Ernesto, where all the characters have to deal with surprise. Each of these scenes can tempt singers to go off course, to mug or ham.

Act II, Scene 2—Introduction and Pasquale's Entrance

The second scene of Act II opens as Pasquale enters, in the full bloom of his obsession. He is not alone: with him comes a servant. From the first act, we know that Pasquale wants his nephew to marry a girl that he, Pasquale, has chosen for him. If Ernesto refuses, he will be disinherited. We also know that Malatesta has arranged to provide a bride for Pasquale (in the Act I, scene 1 aria "Bella siccome un angelo"). He has told Pasquale that this bride is his sister, "Sofronia," and that she has spent most of her life in a convent; he has described her to Pasquale in just enough detail to thoroughly arouse the old man. As he waits for this "sister" to be introduced, Pasquale can revel fully in his expectations (this aria comes in the middle of Act I, scene 2):

Un foco insolito	An unusual fire
Mi sento addosso,	I feel inside me,
Omai resistere	To resist any more
Io più non posso.	I'm no longer able.
Dell'età vecchia	Of old age
Scordo i malanni,	I forget the aches,
Mi sento giovine	I feel young
Come a vent'anni.	Like a twenty-year-old.
Deh! Cara, affrettati!	Oh, dearest, hurry!
Vieni, sposina!	Come, little bride!
Ecco, di bamboli	Here, babies
Mezza dozzina	By the half a dozen,
Già veggo nascere,	Already I see them born,
Già veggo crescere,	Already I see them grown,
A me d'intorno	Around me
Veggo scherzar.	I see them playing.

Like Falstaff in his aria, "Va, vecchio John," Pasquale is entirely consumed by his fantasy: he already sees himself as unstoppably potent, the father of half a dozen children. His own interests preoccupy him; no one else's, such as his nephew's, can be considered. So when Ernesto comes in, Pasquale deals rapidly with him. He offers him once again the girl of his (Pasquale's) choice to marry and then, when Ernesto refuses, throws him out. Not only that, he tells Ernesto that he himself is about to be married. His success so far is clear: not only has he agreeably asserted his authority over his nephew; more important, he has also gotten evidence of his desirability in the bride whom Malatesta has found for him and whom he is just now about to meet. So Pasquale, at the beginning of Act II, scene 2, enters fresh from two triumphs. In practical terms, he is been getting ready to meet this new bride and is full of vigor and excitement.

He enters with a servant to music marked *allegro mosso*. The music for the entrance is not frantic but jocular, perhaps slightly nervous, certainly eager.

(entrando in gran gala; *ed un servo)*	*(entering in grand gala, to a servant* *entering after him)*
Quando avrete introdotto	When you have presented
Il dottor Malatesta	Doctor Malatesta
E chi è con lui,	And the one who is with him,
Ricordatevi bene,	Remember well,
Nessuno ha più d'entrar;	Don't let anyone else enter;
Guai se lasciate rompere	You'll pay for it, if you disobey
La consegna! Adesso andate	My orders! Now go.
(Il servo parte.)	*(The servant leaves.)*
Per un uom sui settanta . . .	For a man in his seventies.
(Zitto, che non mi senta la sposina . . .)	(I don't want my little bride to hear me . . .)
Convien dir che son lesto	I must say that I am agile
E ben portante.	And well preserved.
Con questo boccon poi di toilette . . .	With this dream of a costume . . .
(Pavoneggiandosi)	*(Strutting about like a peacock)*
Alcun viene . . .	Someone is coming . . .
Eccoli.	Here they are.
A te mi raccomando, Imene.	To you I entrust myself, Hymen.

He is going to meet his "sposina" and wants to make a good impression in order to win her. That is his objective in this scene. It is why he is dressed up in his finest clothes, "in gran gala," as the libretto says. What do these clothes look like? Are they old? New? Do they fit? Are they too loose? Too tight? There is laughter to be won by these clothes. But it is essential that they be true to Pasquale's character and to his situation; they must not take over the character. What Pasquale wears must look like what a man in his condition would wear, or would have worn forty years before; they must not be tricked up just to get an easy laugh. They must clearly indicate his objective, carrying all his expectations with them, as well as his obsessiveness. It is there that the humor lies: in the spectacle of an old man dressed up to be the lover he might once have been, and completely unaware of how he appears now. In this way Pasquale simply follows out the logic of his situation; he does not have to try to be funny. Given what we know him to want—his objective for this scene—the worst that could happen is that he might fail to impress his bride. So beneath the bravado that carries his obsession, there is some uncertainty. He is nervous, like a schoolboy on his first date. Almost anything can put him off balance, even so small a thing as his relationship with his servant. How he overcomes these barriers will depend on what he, the director, and the actor playing the servant work out, but there are opportunities here, in this brief moment, for comedy that is based on—that shows—character.

The servant who enters with Pasquale has no lines in the opera (there are three servants in this household, and none of them has any lines) but there are opportunities for comedy nonetheless, all based on the logic of the situation, with no need for hamming. As always, the analysis must be done for everyone in the scene, whether they have many lines, one line, or none. The information available to do the analysis will be indirect, based on clues in the music, on the behavior of others, and on an understanding of servants' traditional roles in nineteenth-century drama and opera. And they will be worked out in detail in rehearsal with the director and the singers. The introduction to the scene lasts ten bars and Pasquale's instructions take another eight bars, so there is enough time for the two of them to build this moment into a small scene together.

Because the role requires no singing, the servant could be played by an actor. Though it is a nonsinging role, it is an extremely important part of the opera—the role is pivotal to the understanding of Pasquale's character.

The servant is coming from the life that goes on outside the opera's visible action, from the life of the Pasquale household and the relationship with his master that has already been established in the opera's first scene. What kind of servants will such a man as Pasquale likely have? Will they be old? Will they have been with him for a long time? Will they be deferential? Familiar? Judgmental? Bored? Each choice carries with it consequences that the servant will project in each of his appearances. We might think, for example, from how we see him behave throughout the course of the opera, that a man like Pasquale will be parsimonious, that he will want a stable home, that he will expect obedience. What kind of servant would such a man have? Likely someone who has been with him for a while, who knows how to deal with him, who may not be well paid but who is too old or too dull to look for better work. Such a servant might have views about what is normal behavior from his master and what is not. Would he express these views directly? Perhaps not, but his views must nonetheless be evident to the audience in the expression on his face and in his body's movements or posture. They will also be evident to Pasquale, since Pasquale has lines showing that he is reacting to his servant. The servant is going to do what Pasquale has told him to do—to show Dr. Malatesta and the person who is with him in and to keep anyone else out. He may want to express his disapproval of his master's fancy clothes and fancy intentions. He may be confused and bewildered by the unexpected developments and wanting things to get back to normal. Or he may simply be lethargic, uninterested in anything that is going on. He may show his disapproval behind Pasquale's back by putting a sour expression on his face or by walking slowly. He may walk slowly because he is trying to puzzle things out. Or he may lag behind because that is what he always does. Pasquale may be aware of his disapproval—or confusion, or lethargy—from the beginning, or he may realize it quickly as the brief scene unfolds, but he must see something so that his response will have a focus. That means the person playing the servant must give his master something to react to. But these choices will be appropriate to the character that the actor and the director agree on; they will not be mugging. While the servant will have to obey his master, for example, he need not show that he approves. He may dawdle on his way out of the room, he may give Pasquale a look of scorn, he may make some sign of derision, confusion, or impatience. Pasquale may or may not see this—perhaps not, in fact, since he so quickly turns to thinking of the impression he is going to make. Whichever reaction is chosen, it must fit with the character of the servant that is being worked out in rehearsal. There are many opportunities for comedy here.

Stanislavsky's "there are not small parts, only small actors" is particularly appropriate in opera. There are many small nonsinging roles in various operas that are crucial to the action. These scenes need a great deal of attention.

A scene must have conflict, even a short one like this, and the conflict has to be overcome. The sign that there is conflict between the two—and that it is resolved, for the time being at least—is in the way Pasquale concludes his order-giving: "Guai se lasciate rompere la consegna!" (You'll pay for it, if you don't obey my orders!)

Once the servant has left, Pasquale takes stock of himself. Why? And how? Why does he suddenly admit his age—"Per un uom sui settanta" (For a man in his seventies)? Is he for a moment insecure? Why might he be? Could the brief scene with his servant have made him uneasy? If he is insecure, he quickly compensates, finding a compliment for himself: "Convien dir che son lesto e ben portante" (I must say that I am agile and well preserved). His mind is working, perhaps building defenses, perhaps instilling confidence. We in the audience should be able to see his thoughts. He thinks of his clothes with delight: "Con questo boccon poi di toilette" (With this dream of a costume). There is a stage direction in the Ricordi score that reads "pavoneggiandosi" (strutting about preening himself). Stage directions are tricky. Anyone could have written them—the composer, the librettist, a director or singer, even the publisher. What is important is that the singer try to understand the spirit of the direction, and this one is not so difficult.

Stage directions are usually descriptions, for example "passionately," "gloomily," "cheerfully," but these descriptions are not helpful in playing a scene. In fact, they cannot really be played except in the most generalized terms. Only actions can be played, and when those active moments are specific, we in the audience see the results. The only way to find actions is through verb choices. "Pavoneggiandosi" happens to be very helpful verb.

The stage direction "pavoneggiandosi" suggests is a kind of arrogance: for a man of nearly seventy to look so good, to feel so powerful, is a wonderful thing, in that man's mind. And this kind of arrogance suits the comedy's logic: to show Pasquale puffing himself up prepares us for his eventual deflation. The playing of comedy demands more intensity and focus than do the other forms: the stakes are higher here than in, say, a tragedy, because they are more artificial.

Suddenly there is a noise. Pasquale realizes that Malatesta and the young woman are here. He makes a final plea to Hymen—the Roman god of marriage—to whom he entrusts his success. This is followed by a fermata, a moment of silence as Pasquale waits. In this moment, what does Pasquale do? Does he look nervously toward the door? Does he look away? Is he frozen in anxiety? What is going through his mind? Is he wondering how to conduct himself—should he bow, for example, or stay aloof, or play the charming and hospitable host?

ACT II, SCENE 3—PRESENTATION OF "SOFRONIA"

The key changes. It is more somber, even portentous. There are two strong chords, and the new scene begins. There is another fermata. Malatesta brings in his "sister," the bride-to be, whom he is calling "Sofronia"; we know she is really Norina in disguise. But before we can see how the three characters could behave, we should know more about Malatesta and Norina.

First Malatesta. By this point we know pretty much all we need to about him. We know he is the master of the plots. He can be so because he is trusted by everyone (although Ernesto has some painful moments thinking Malatesta has betrayed him). We know that, as Pasquale's confidant, he has arranged to act as a kind of marriage broker for the old man; that he has "found" a suitable young woman for him, the very one he is bringing in now; and that, to increase Pasquale's confidence (and eagerness), he is claiming the young woman is his sister. We know as well, from his asides in Act I, scene 2 and his conversation with Norina in Act I, scene 5, that he thinks Pasquale is a fool for wanting to marry a young woman, that in reality he is Ernesto's friend, and that he is plotting to bring Ernesto and his beloved, Norina, together. (Norina is of course also the woman who is playing the part of the innocent sister, the woman Pasquale is to marry.) We have seen him provide Norina with very careful directions, in Act I, scene 5, the end of the first act, for how to behave as "Sofronia." Norina wonders if she should be "fiera" (haughty) or "mesta" (sad); if she should "piangere" (weep) or "gridare" (scream). Malatesta says no, none of that: she should "convien far la semplicetta" (play the simple little girl), "collo torto, bocca stretta" (neck twisted, mouth narrow).

His instructions are precise and Norina picks them up quickly. Where Malatesta is coming from, then, is from having prepped Norina for her role as "Sofronia," the shy and innocent bride-to-be. He is going to introduce "Sofronia" to Pasquale. And he wants to intensify Pasquale's eagerness to the point where he will agree to marry this young woman on the spot. Several things might prevent him from getting what he wants: Pasquale may become suspicious; he might want to give himself time for second thoughts; he might be assailed by common sense and realize that no young woman could want to marry a man so old as he; he may begin to think about his money instead of his desire. For any or all of these reasons, he may change his mind and decide not to go through with the marriage. So Malatesta will have to be on his toes: he must make sure that Pasquale's attention is focused on "Sofronia," that his interest is heated up to the point where there is no room in his mind for sense.

When we first see Norina in Act I, scene 4, she is reading, and laughing at, a romance novel. She is laughing because she sees through its mawkish conventions, for example that of the amorous glance that the lady gives her lover, which causes him to fall dazed to his knees: "E tanto era in quel guardo sapor di paradiso" (And there was in that look a taste of paradise). Yet she also knows how to exploit these conventions: "So anch'io la virtù magica d'un guardo a tempo e loco" (I know also the magical virtue of a glance at the right time and place). And she runs through a catalog of them, of which, she says, she is the mistress. But, she insists, "Ho testa bizzarra, ma core eccellente" (I've a capricious head, but an excellent heart). (She says this, and we know that Ernesto believes it, but is it true? Her actions in the rest of the opera will have to show us.) Just before Malatesta gets there, she is given a note from Ernesto telling her that he has been evicted because Pasquale is going to marry Malatesta's sister and he, Ernesto, is therefore going away. This surprises and saddens her, so when Malatesta gets there to give her the details of the plot to dupe Pasquale—so that she can marry Ernesto—she refuses to participate anymore; with her lover exiled, there is no point. Malatesta needs to convince her that Ernesto will not leave. This short but highly charged scene has high stakes. She has to be persuaded that she need not worry, that Ernesto will be all right. Malatesta then tells her his plan and teaches her how to behave so that the plot will work, as we saw above. So where she is coming from, as she enters the room to meet Don Pasquale, is from having been prepared by Malatesta to play her role so convincingly that the old man will not be able to stop himself from marrying her. But she has also been careful to establish her moral bona fides: she tells Malatesta that she is only going to do this because "Pronto io son; purch'io non manchi all'amore del caro bene" (I am ready, as long as I don't disappoint the love of my dear one). At the end of Act I, scene 5, therefore, we know four things: Norina is capable of deceit; even so, she wants us to know she has a good heart; she is willing to participate in deceit in order to win Ernesto; and she really does want to win Ernesto. She is ready to play the role of Malatesta's sister, the shy and virtuous maiden, "Sofronia," heavily veiled and "fresca uscita di convento" (newly arrived from the convent). She is ready to tell Don Pasquale what he wants to hear and make him fall in love with and marry her, deeding half his worldly goods over to her on the spot. That is her objective. The main obstacle, or risk, is Pasquale himself, who may not like her, or who may not believe her performance, or who may suddenly think of his money. To conquer Pasquale—the immediate challenge—she has to perform so convincingly and invitingly that he has no time for second thoughts.

So the stakes are high for each of the players. Each is on the verge of getting what he or she wants; for each, success will ensure his or her happiness—or so they think.

Back to the action. We have heard the change in key, the two strong chords, and the second fermata. What happens?

Here is one scenario. On the two chords, the servant opens the door. On the second fermata, Pasquale looks quickly through the door: he thinks he sees two figures but cannot quite make out who they are, so he looks again. Then, as the music begins again, we see Malatesta pulling a heavily veiled Norina through the door. That is why the music begins: it takes its cue from the entrances of Malatesta and Norina. The music is syncopated, off the beat, as if to suggest Norina's hesitation. She stops at the doorway, and this, in turn, cues Malatesta to say, "Via, coraggio" (Come now, courage). Norina feigns weakness: "Reggo appena. Tremo tutta" (I can barely stand. I'm all atremble). This is all for Pasquale's benefit. To her, Malatesta says,

"V'inoltrate" (Come in further). Then he turns toward Pasquale, as the direction in the libretto has it, and gestures to him to move a little out of the way to prevent Norina from seeing him. This, in turn, motivates Norina's little cry: "Ah, fratel, non mi lasciate" (Ah, brother, don't leave me). Why does Malatesta ask Pasquale to move out of Norina's sight? There is an obvious reason: it is to intensify the tease, increase Pasquale's curiosity, perhaps make him feel a little awkward or uncertain—all to raise the stakes even higher.

This is a tempting moment. The singers playing Malatesta and Norina may be tempted to do some business of their own: wink at the audience, nudge each other, make faces—trying to show how absurd the scene is, to get the audience on their side, and with luck to get a laugh. But it might be a laugh totally out of the context of the scene. The temptation must be resisted.

What singers sometimes do, when they try to get a laugh, is express an opinion about what their character is doing; they tell us in the audience how absurd that character or the situation is, and how well they know it is absurd. In effect, they set themselves outside and above their characters or the situation. They are commenting (making an observation or explanation about the situation) or editorializing (giving an opinion of the situation or the character). But this scene is absurd only if it works in its own reality, logically, as it has been written to do, and it works only if Malatesta and his "sister" stay focused on their objectives. If the singers playing these characters use their entrance to do their own business, the logic will be broken. For example: the logic requires them—and us in the audience—to at least consider the possibility that they could fail. If there is no possibility that they could fail, there is no suspense. If there is no suspense, why should we pay attention? Winks and nudges from the singers have nothing to do with the characters they are playing or with the logic of the scene; they are attempts to ingratiate themselves with their audience, but we in the audience will not find it charming. Our sympathies will move away from Malatesta and Norina toward Pasquale; we might even become a little annoyed at them. There will be moments, soon, when Malatesta and Norina as characters can express their double nature; Donizetti has given them these moments. But not just now.

The six bars that follow their entrance let us see Malatesta cross back to Norina to try to calm her. "Non temete," he says (Don't be afraid). In fact, he says it two more times, three times in all, because Norina says, "Per pietà" (For pity's sake), three times. Malatesta has got Pasquale to move away, presumably so that he does not frighten the girl from the convent and also, no doubt, to increase his interest. Pasquale will probably try to steal some furtive glimpses and overhear her conversation with her "brother." Under her first "Per pietà," the marking in the orchestra is *accelerando*; this increase in tempo directs her display of terror, which is, of course, for Pasquale's sake. After her third little cry, Malatesta leaves her again and crosses to Pasquale to explain her behavior. He is very busy directing the scene; part of our pleasure, in the audience, is watching his skill at doing this. He tells Pasquale:

Fresca uscita di convento,	Newly arrived from the convent,
Naturale è il turbamento;	It's only natural that she is confused;
Per natura un po' selvatica,	By nature a bit timid,
Mansuefarla a voi si sta.	It's up to you to make her blossom.

That is pretty exciting for an eager old man to hear, the implication of the rather surprising verb "mansuefarla" (tame) being that he will be able to do pretty much what he wants with her. It leads directly to a trio:

NORINA *(a parte)*	NORINA *(to herself)*
Sta a vedere, vecchio matto,	It's obvious, crazy fool,
Ch'or ti servo come va, *ecc.*	I'll show you how it goes, *etc.*
PASQUALE, MALATESTA	PASQUALE, MALATESTA
Mosse . . . voce . . . portamento,	Gestures . . . voice . . . bearing,
Tutto è in lei semplicità, *ecc.*	All is in her simplicity, *etc.*
PASQUALE	PASQUALE
La dichiaro un gran portento,	I'll declare she's a great miracle,
Se risponde la beltà, *ecc.*	If that beauty responds to me , *etc.*

The trio is like punctuation: it lets the characters express together where each of them is in the scene. At this point, it is important that Malatesta and Pasquale be close together and Norina somewhat apart. The way the trio is structured suggests that there is a dialogue between the two men: Malatesta is feeding Pasquale with the idea of Norina's "semplicità," and Pasquale is picking it all up eagerly. But Donizetti gives Norina, separately, the chance to express her double nature. The way he has written her vocal line (in "ch'or ti servo come va") dictates her attitude: he has given her runs of sixteenth and dotted sixteenth notes, in a rhythm suggesting laughter, then little groups of four 32nd-note runs suggesting that she is unable to hold her laughter in. Her mocking thoughts are an aside to herself; in the score, they are bracketed. They make perfect sense: she has just had her first sight of Pasquale, the man whose folly and obsession are preventing her from marrying the man she loves, so it is logical that she should be annoyed, and that she should express that annoyance to herself. But she is expressing this as Norina, not as the singer playing Norina. She is staying within the logic of her character, and she is supported—even directed—by Donizetti in doing so.

It is she who ends the trio and calls Malatesta back to her. He crosses the stage again and tries to reassure her:

NORINA
Ah fratello!

NORINA
Ah brother!

MALATESTA
Non temete, non temete.

MALATESTA
Don't be afraid, don't be afraid.

NORINA
A star sola mi fa male.

NORINA
To be alone makes me uneasy.

MALATESTA
Cara mia, sola non siete;
Ci son io, c'e Don Pasquale.

MALATESTA
My dear, you're not alone;
I'm here, there's Don Pasquale.

NORINA
Come? un uom? Ah, me
  meschina!
Presto, andiamo, fuggiam
  di qua!

NORINA
What? A man? Ah, woe
  is me!
Quick, let's leave, let's run away from
  here!

MALATESTA
Coraggio, non temete!

MALATESTA
Courage, don't be afraid!

PASQUALE
Dottore!
Com'è cara, com'è cara!

PASQUALE
Doctor!
How dear she is, how dear she is!

As they play this short scene, Norina and Malatesta must be acutely aware of how Pasquale is responding to their performance. How do they show their awareness? Does Malatesta look back at the old man? Norina must not; she must keep her head bowed, in her character as the fearful virgin. When he tells her there is a man present, perhaps she reaches out to touch his hand, to make him come closer; perhaps she half turns away, as if to move toward the door. But all the time they are paying attention to Pasquale, and, as if on cue, he delivers the words they need to hear. He is following his own objective, which is to acquire a lovely, biddable young bride. And this leads to another trio, another point of punctuation in the action of the scene:

NORINA
Sta' a vedere, vecchio matto, *ecc.*

PASQUALE
Com'è cara, modestina
Nella sua semplicità! *ecc.*

MALATESTA
Com'è scaltra, malandrina!
Impazzire lo farà! *ecc.*

NORINA
Oh! fratello!
Tremo tutta!
(a parte)
Sta' a vedere, *ecc.*

NORINA
He's gawking the, silly old fool, *etc.*

PASQUALE
How adorable she is! How modest,
So modest in her artlessness! *etc.*

MALATESTA
How artful she is, the little rogue!
She'll drive him crazy! *etc.*

NORINA
Oh, brother!
I'm all of a tremble!
(aside)
He's gawking, *etc.*

This time it is Norina and Malatesta who are together and Pasquale who is left alone, in a state of anticipatory rapture. Both men profess their admiration of Norina, but with a difference, Malatesta's word for Norina, "scaltra" (artful), being the opposite of Pasquale's "semplicità" (artlessness). The comments of Malatesta and Norina are marked in the score as asides. They could be played to each other, which might make the remarks more interesting than playing them vaguely into the air. Some could be played to each other and some alone. But they must not be vague. Malatesta's praise is spoken, obviously, in his "real" character, not the character he is pretending to be for Pasquale. It is spoken entirely within the logic of what he has to do; there is no mugging needed. Norina repeats her contempt for Pasquale, with (as before) the reminder to us of who she really is and how she will behave once the plot has succeeded. As before, in the first trio, the music leads her. In the middle of the trio, Malatesta must again move toward Pasquale, joining him both musically and textually. It seems that things are going well so far, but Malatesta and Norina must not assume the scene is over: they must still draw Pasquale along to the point where he will sign the wedding agreement. So Malatesta thinks it is time for him to bring Norina a little closer to the old man, and even get them talking.

The scene continues, with more pressure being applied. Each new bit of pressure requires great care: Malatesta and Norina must each see that Pasquale is responding as they want him to. They must be neither too quick nor too slow, their timing dictated at each step by his responses. At all times, Malatesta watches Pasquale and manages the stages. He speeds him up, then slows him down: he makes Pasquale want Norina to take off her veil, but then, to whet his appetite even more, tries to get him to back off:

Non oseria, son certo,	She wouldn't dare, I am certain
A sembiante scoperto	With an uncovered face
Parlare a un uom.	Talk to a man.
Prima l'interrogate,	First ask her questions,
Vedete se nei gusti v'incontrate	See if your tastes are complementary.
Poscia vedrem.	Then we'll see.

So Pasquale tries to talk to her. But it has been so long since he has spoken to a lady, especially one he is trying to impress, that he can hardly form a sentence.

(Capisco, andiam, coraggio.)	(I understand, let's go, courage.)
(a Norina)	*(to Norina)*
Posto che ho l'avvantaggio . . .	Since I have the honor . . .
(s'imbroglia)	*(getting his words mixed up)*
Anzi il signor fratello . . .	In fact, the mister brother . . .
Il dottor Malatesta . . .	Doctor Malatesta . . .
Cio è voleva dir . . .	That is, I meant to say . . .

Malatesta sees this: "Perde la testa," he says (He's losing his head), and so he gets Norina to help him: "Son serva. Mille grazie," she says (I am your servant. A thousand thanks). This is exactly what an obedient young wife-to-be should say. (While Pasquale is reaching for his words, does he turn away? If so, maybe Malatesta and Norina can turn to each other. It should go without saying that Pasquale must not see this.) Encouraged, he asks his questions: Do you like company in the evening? Do you like to go to the theater? How do you like to pass your time? Her answers are, of course, satisfactory: at the convent we were always alone; I do not know what the theater is and I don't want to; we were always busy sewing, embroidering, knitting, and seeing to the cooking.

There are several ways to play this scene. The choices come from its rhythms. If both Norina and Pasquale play in the same tempo, there will be no tension. It is easy for two characters in a scene to pick up on each other's rhythms. But that takes away contrast, and therefore loosens dramatic tension. If Pasquale's comments and questions are slow and deliberate, then Norina's must be quick and sharp. If the reverse is true, then more of Norina's reluctance can be displayed. In either case, Norina must be impressive, in order to earn the reactions she gets from both men. "Ah, malandrina!" cries Malatesta, aside (Oh you little rogue!). "Fa proprio al caso mio" (She's just what I want), says Pasquale. This remark is also marked as an aside, but it could be addressed either to Malatesta or to himself. The singer might well ask whom he is addressing: if it is himself, then he is confirming that she is a perfect mate; if Malatesta, then he is confirming that the doctor has done well. In any case, it is time for his reward: the unveiling.

Donizetti sets the moment up beautifully. Up to this point he has let the recitative of questions and responses pass with very little accompaniment, allowing Pasquale and Norina complete freedom in their delivery. So they can speak very consciously to each other, each absorbing what the other has to say and responding without the dictates of strict bar lines—pure acting. This spareness is in stunning contrast to the entry of the orchestra when the veil comes off. It is like an explosion, and that is exactly the way Pasquale experiences it:

PASQUALE	PASQUALE
Una bomba in mezzo al core.	A bomb in the middle of my heart.
Per carità, dottore,	For pity's sake, doctor,
Ditele se mi vuole.	Ask her if she'll have me.
Mi mancan le parole,	Words fail me,
Sudo ... agghiaccio ... son morto.	I sweat ... I'm in a chill ... dying.

Now Malatesta knows he has hooked his big old fish. But can he land him?

MALATESTA	MALATESTA
Via, coraggio,	Come, courage.
Mi sembra ben disposta:	She seems agreeable to me:
Ora le parlo.	Now I'll talk to her.

Malatesta can play this response in several ways. He can be calm and dispassionate, like a calm brother and friend. He can be enthusiastic, sharing Pasquale's excitement. Or he can feign reluctance at giving his "sister" to Pasquale. Whatever the choice, the point is to force Pasquale to commit himself.

(a Norina)	(to Norina)
Sorellina mia cara,	My dear little sister,
Dite ... vorreste ... in breve,	Tell me ... would you like ... in short,
Quel signore vi piace?	This gentleman ... does he appeal to you?
NORINA	NORINA
A dirlo ho soggezione ...	I feel too uneasy to say it ...
MALATESTA	MALATESTA
Coraggio.	Courage.
NORINA	NORINA
Sì.	Yes.

Norina's one word, "Sì," is the climax of the scene, the point toward which all Malatesta's and Norina's plots have been leading. But things are not over yet. They have to get in a notary, make an agreement of marriage, and get the old man to sign it; and they have to do all this quickly in case he changes his mind. Outside, waiting, is the Notary, who, as Malatesta told Norina earlier in Act I, scene 2, is his cousin. Malatesta brings him in; Pasquale dictates terms that are agreeable to all, endowing Norina with half his worldly goods; the papers are signed, and everything seems fixed.

But there is a block—two, really. "Non vedo i testimoni. Un solo non può star" (I do not see the witnesses. One alone will not do), says the Notary. At that point there is a commotion outside the door: it is Ernesto trying to get in. "Ernesto!" says Malatesta, "e non sa niente!" (Ernesto! And he doesn't know anything!). The plotters face a big risk: that Ernesto, who knows nothing of their scheme, and who can be expected to be very suspicious on seeing Norina about to marry his uncle, will spoil it all.

ACT II, SCENES 4 AND 5—ENTRY OF ERNESTO

Where has Ernesto been? And why has he been left out of the plot? The audience will no doubt be as surprised to see him as anyone onstage.

We last saw him alone, at the beginning of the second act. His recitative and aria, "Povero Ernesto" (Poor Ernesto), open the second act. They follow directly after Act I, scene 5 (the last scene in Act I), where Malatesta teaches Norina how to play the simple, innocent girl, and precede Act II, scene 2, the entry of Pasquale in his courting attire. It seems that the action of the opera is passing Ernesto by. And that is a problem, both for the director and for the singer playing Ernesto: he can seem to lack definition, even to be somewhat passive. At the opening of Act II he reflects on his situation.

Povero Ernesto!	Poor Ernesto!
Dallo zia cacciato,	Thrown out by my uncle,
Da tutti abbandonato,	All have abandoned me,
Mi restava un amico,	There remained to me one friend,
E un coperto nemico	And an enemy in disguise
Discopro in lui,	I discover in him,
Che a danni miei congiura.	Who is plotting my downfall.
Perder Norina, oh Dio!	To lose Norina, oh God!
Ben feci a le d'esprimere	I did well to explain
In un foglio i sensi miei.	In a letter my sentiments to her.
Ora in altra contrada	Now in some other land
I giorni grami a trascinar si vada.	Let me drag out my wretched days.
Cercherò lontana terra	I will search for a far-off land
Dove gemer sconosciuto,	Where, to moan unknown,
Là vivrò col cuore in guerra	I will live, with my heart at war

Deplorando il ben perduto, ecc.	Lamenting my lost beloved, etc.
Ma nè sorte a me nemica,	But neither fate, which is my enemy,
Nè frapposti monti e mar,	Nor the seas and mountains between us,
Ti potranno, dolce amica,	Will be able, sweet friend,
Dal mio core cancellar, ecc.	To erase you from my heart, etc.
E se fia che ad altro oggetto	And if it happens that to another love
Tu rivolga un giorno il core	You should someday give your heart,
Se mai fia	If ever it happens
Che un nuovo affetto	That a new affection
Spegna in te l'antico ardore,	Should extinguish in you the old flame,
Non temer che un infelice	Fear not that this unhappy man
Te spergiura accusi al ciel;	Will accuse you to heaven of perjury;
Se tu sei, ben mio, felice,	If you are, my love, happy,
Sarà pago il tuo fedel, ecc.	Your faithful one will be satisfied, etc.
Cercherò lontana terra, ecc.	I will search for a far-off land, etc.

The recitative recapitulates the facts: Ernesto has been thrown out and disinherited by his uncle for refusing the woman Pasquale insisted he marry; he thinks he has been betrayed by his friend, Malatesta (though he does not know that the woman intended for his uncle is in fact Norina); and he has written honorably to Norina to break off their relationship, since he feels he cannot ask her to marry a pauper. In the aria he comments on this and sorts out his feelings, which are noble and generous. Perhaps they could seem a little overly so. Why has he not, for example, confronted Malatesta? Why has he not he asked Norina what she would like? (Ernesto can be thought of, here, as behaving a little like a character in the kind of romance Norina was reading when we first met her, at which she was laughing.) In any case, because Ernesto is alone and therefore has no need to grandstand or play for sympathy, we can take his sentiments for the truth. The challenge in the aria is to show Ernesto becoming active, not just the recipient of others' decisions, but vital and assertive in himself. This, to some extent, it does. It begins with a slow section of four bars, as if he were calming himself down after reviewing his situation. As it becomes clear to him that, while he will never forget Norina, he can accept that she may find someone else to love, and that he will accept that as long as she is happy, the tempo increases. The aria ends differently than it began, with Ernesto determined and resolved.

So Ernesto is coming see his uncle for one last time. What does he want? He says:

Pria di partir, signore	Before leaving, sir,
Vengo per dirvi addio,	I come to say goodbye,
E come un malfattore	And like a malefactor
Mi vien conteso entrar!	I am prevented from entering!

So it seems he only wants—again honorably—to say goodbye to his uncle. But the servants outside the door try to stop him getting in. They are only obeying Pasquale, who at the beginning of Act I, scene 2 told them not to let anyone in. Ernesto battles with them and ends up forcing his way into the room. He says he has been treated like "un malfattore" (a criminal). The singer playing Ernesto can speculate. Am I only trying to say goodbye? If so, why do I fight with them to get in? Or do I want to say a few sharp things to my uncle? Am I hoping that, faced with the reality of my departure, my uncle will change his mind? Or am I so angry at this treatment that I am now angry at him? Whatever the choice is, Ernesto shows that he has some spunk, not fully revealed before. And that informs his objective, which is, simply, to confront his uncle, for one reason or another, one last time.

His entry earns him a gratifying amount of attention, but it also creates a crisis. Not for Pasquale, who is able to maintain his objective: to get the marriage contract signed and the marriage itself under way. But Malatesta and Norina have to adapt quickly. Whereas their objectives had been quite straightforward—to get Pasquale to commit himself to "Sofronia"—their tactics have not been; they have depended on role playing and deception. Now someone has appeared who knows who Norina really is and, moreover, has an intense and special interest in her. What are they to do? While they listen to Ernesto outside the door, battling with the servants, they will be busy: first dealing with their shock, then trying to decide what to do:

NORINA
Ernesto!

MALATESTA
Ernesto! e non sa niente;

NORINA
Or veramente mi viene da tremar!

ERNESTO
Indietro,

MALATESTA
Ernesto può tutto rovinar!

ERNESTO
Io voglio entrar,

PASQUALE
Mio nipote!

NORINA
Ernesto!

MALATESTA
Ernesto! and he doesn't know a thing;

NORINA
Now truly I am trembling!

ERNESTO
Out of my way,

MALATESTA
Ernesto can ruin everything!

ERNESTO
I want to come in,

PASQUALE
My nephew!

MALATESTA	MALATESTA
E non sa niente.	And he knows nothing.
ERNESTO	ERNESTO
Mascalzoni.	Scoundrels.
NORINA E MALATESTA	NORINA AND MALATESTA
Or tutto veramente	Now everything surely
Ci viene a rovinar!	Will be destroyed!

At the end of this ensemble, there are three bars of conclusion. The next section has a brief dialogue between Ernesto and Pasquale. There is no mention of Malatesta or Norina, and this suggests that they are physically out of Ernesto's sight. They could be out of his sight by chance, by arrangement of the furniture, or by choice—deliberately hiding from him, hoping Pasquale will quickly dismiss him. As they listen to the dialogue, they have to figure out their next actions. They could try to stay hidden until Ernesto leaves, they could appear and try to brave it out, or they could try to escape. The audience will be able to see them deciding what to do. It is Pasquale who gives them away by insisting that Ernesto meet his new bride:

PASQUALE	PASQUALE
S'era in faccende giunto	You arrived and interrupted our business
Però voi siete in punto.	But you are in time
A fare il matrimonio	To complete the marriage
Mancava un testimonio.	We were missing a witness.
Giunto voi siete in punto.	You arrived at the right time.
(volgendosi a Norina)	*(turning to Norina)*
Or venga la sposina.	My little bride, approach.
ERNESTO	ERNESTO
Che vedo?	What's this I see?
MALATESTA	MALATESTA
Per carità,	For pity's sake,
ERNESTO	ERNESTO
O ciel,	Oh heavens,
MALATESTA	MALATESTA
. . . sta zitto, . . .	be quiet,
ERNESTO	ERNESTO
. . . Norina! . . .	Norina!
MALATESTA	MALATESTA
. . . ci vuoi precipitar. . . .	do you want to ruin everything.

The time between Pasquale's introduction and Ernesto's first sight of Norina is very short. The bar in which he actually sees Norina is marked *poco meno*, which gives some time for the moments of surprise and recognition to be played: as he sees her, Ernesto blurts out, on a *fortissimo*, "Che vedo?" (What do I see?). In that one phrase, Malatesta must get physically close to Ernesto and try to control him, stop him from giving the whole game away, even though there is no time for him to explain to Ernesto just exactly what the whole game is. At the same time, whatever his actions are, they must not be seen by Pasquale, who might be occupied in shuffling legal papers with the notary, nor must Pasquale hear Ernesto address "Sofronia" as Norina.

The stakes are very high, the highest they have been in the opera. Do the objectives of Malatesta and Norina change? No: they still want to get Pasquale to sign the marriage contract. But they absolutely must have new intentions. The action has forced on them an almost complete change of direction, a reversal: from being in control of the situation, managing Pasquale's behavior, they are suddenly at the mercy of something unpredicted and unpredictable. The challenge for them is to get back some kind of control. Ernesto, too, is facing the unexpected; nothing has prepared him for the sight of his beloved Norina and his former friend in the house of his uncle, much less for the idea that his beloved is going to become his uncle's bride. Does he have a new objective? Yes: he now has to understand this extraordinary event. There is a quartet in which each character expresses his feelings:

NORINA
Adesso veramente
Mi viene da tremare,
Sì, sì, mi viene, *ecc.*

NORINA
Now truly
I'm beginning to tremble,
Oh yes, I'm beginning, *etc.*

ERNESTO
Sofronia! sua sorella!
Comincio ad impazzare,
Sì, sì, comincio, *ecc.*

ERNESTO
Sofronia his sister!
I'm starting to go crazy,
Yes, yes, I must be, *etc.*

PASQUALE
Gli punge, compatitelo,
Io vo' capacitare,
Sì, sì, la vo', *ecc.*

PASQUALE
He's stung, have pity on him,
I want to make him understand,
Yes, I want to, *etc.*

MALATESTA
Figliuol, non mi far scene, *ecc.*
È tutto per tuo bene, *ecc.*
Se vuoi Norina perdere
Hai che seguitar, *ecc.*

MALATESTA
Ah, my son, don't make a scene, *etc.*
All is for your own good, *etc.*
If you want to lose Norina
Keep it up, *etc.*

Seconda la commedia,	Help the comedy,
Lascia far, sì, lascia far, *ecc.*	Yes, let it go, *etc.*

After the quartet, there is a fermata: it is the moment in which Ernesto has to decide whether or not to reveal that "Sofronia" is Norina, not Malatesta's sister. But obviously he is unprepared: as far as he knows, it is Malatesta who has betrayed him in Act II. What can Malatesta do, rapidly, to convince him to witness the contract? He has time to say only a few words; he cannot properly fill Ernesto in. Does Ernesto give in simply to satisfy Donizetti's need for the plot to work out the way he wants? Even if that is all Donizetti was thinking about, the singer still has to find a way to play the moment. For him to remain quiet at this point requires an almost complete reversal of his very recent aggressive behavior in forcing his way into his uncle's house. In fact, it will be the second reversal for him, both experienced very close together. What makes him accept this one? Is he simply so surprised that he is speechless? Or taken aback by Norina's dress? Or might some intuition warn him that, since he does not have the full story, he had better keep his peace? If that is the choice made, then it must follow logically from the way Malatesta deals with him. And that is a big challenge: Malatesta has only a few seconds and not many words to convince him that he is sincere and really working in his interest.

But the reversals are not over: to come is the greatest of all. The contract has been signed; Ernesto has somehow been made to witness it; and now Pasquale, logically, expects to be able to enjoy his new young bride:

PASQUALE	PASQUALE
Mi sento liquefar.	I feel as if I'm melting!
(cercando di abbracciarla)	*(trying to embrace Norina)*
Carina!	Darling!
NORINA	NORINA
(riprendendo il suo contegno naturale)	*(throwing off her simpering role)*
Adagio un poco:	Not so fast:
Calmate quel gran foco.	Cool your great passion.
Si chiede pria licenza.	One would ask permission first.
PASQUALE	PASQUALE
Me l'accordate?	Will you grant it to me?
NORINA	NORINA
No.	No.
ERNESTO	ERNESTO
Ah! ah! ah! ah!	Ha ha! Ha ha!

It is a brilliant piece of dramaturgy. A simple "No," and the whole plot turns 180 degrees. The "No" is followed by a fermata. In the fermata awareness jells. Ernesto finally realizes what is going on (perhaps Norina glances at him, as if to underline the moment?): hence his laugh. Malatesta can step back and watch as she steps out of her role as "semplicità." Norina knows that she is free to do what she has to do now, which is to assert complete control over Pasquale, to make him so fed up with her that he will eagerly agree to an annulment. She also knows that this will require insults and painful moments for the old man.

But for Pasquale the fermata leads only to questions, not recognition; he is just at the beginning of *his* reversals. He has approached his new wife to embrace her; he has been told to slow down and ask permission; he has asked permission; and he has been refused. Then he has heard his nephew, whom he had so brusquely dismissed, laugh. Having been led by Malatesta—and by "Sofronia" herself—to believe that his bride would be entirely controllable, he must wonder what is going on. What does he do? Is he lost in disbelief? Is he so startled that he can do nothing? We've seen earlier how quick-tempered he is; does he lose his temper now? He says to Ernesto:

Che c'è da ridere, impertinente?	What's so funny, you impertinent twerp?
Partite subito, immantinente,	Leave at once, immediately,
Va, fuor di casa.	Leave this house.

If anger is chosen, then his words to Ernesto will of course be angry ones. If it is disbelief, then they will be full of confusion. Or do we see just a flash of anger, not directed at Norina but at his nephew? Her response is to contradict him: to tell Ernesto to stay, and to promise to teach Pasquale better manners. The scene develops rapidly as she insults, provokes, and browbeats him. She calls him fat and gross; she laughs at his having only three servants, then doubles their wages and promises to hire more servants; she announces she will buy more furniture; she demands to see the hairdresser, the seamstress, and the jeweler—her demands go on and on as her demeanor hardens. Pasquale cannot stop her, though he tries. Defeated, he is reduced to sputtering; now he and everyone else know what is going on.

For Pasquale there are more reversals to come. And the only recognition he is allowed is that he is a victim. It is only at the very end of the opera, after he has been humiliated in every way—economically, domestically, and sexually—that he catches a glimpse of what he should have known at the beginning: that it is the role of old men to get out of the way when love is on the march. Nature, after all, does have its laws.

Comedy has its laws as well. Surprise and its consequences—reversal and recognition—are its essence. But they will work only if the singers (and the director) respect the logic of what the opera invites them to do and, by working together, create a world that fulfills that logic.

Tragedy: Tchaikovsky, *Eugene Onegin*, Act III, Scenes 1–2

If comedy has its logic, and it is the logic that has to be played, not the comedy, the same can be said of tragedy. In comedy, the logic is very serious. It begins with the rigid position that a particular character takes to get what he wants, but that also makes him absurd; in the world of the comedy this absurdity is exposed, and characters who are not rigid find ways to come together and form a new society. In tragedy it is the opposite: the logic is open, vigorous, expectant—at least for a while. That is why Violetta in *La traviata* is giving a party: because she is looking ahead, to more parties, more life; what she is *not* doing is always looking for her handkerchief. It is why Lear divides his kingdom: so he can live life on his own terms, well loved, free from responsibility. It is why Oedipus takes it upon himself to solve the plague of Thebes: so he can exult once more in his heroic nature, the nature that once before killed the bully at the crossroads and mastered the Sphinx. Failure and death ensue because no one, not Violetta, not Lear, not Oedipus, can command reality, or the gods. But at the beginning they think they can, they *want* to, and it is their clamorous will to live that is most evident.

If a singer begins a tragedy by playing the sadness, there is no place to go when the sadness finally comes. It is also in tragedy where the need for humor is most demanding.

Tchaikovsky began work on *Onegin* in May of 1877; by the following February it was finished. Some scenes were performed in December 1878 by students at the Moscow Conservatory, where he was teaching. Finally, on January 23, 1881, the whole piece was mounted at the Bolshoi Theater with a professional cast.

The opera is based on Pushkin's verse novel *Yevgeny Onegin*. Tchaikovsky wanted scenes done at the Conservatory before the whole opera was given a professional production because he knew that Pushkin's poem was revered, and that any attempt to meddle with it or being seen as trying to rival it would be viewed with hostility. So he was eager to establish his version on its own terms. The opera's full name is *Eugene Onegin: Lyrical Scenes in Three Acts*—is a complement to Pushkin, not something that in any way would challenge him. As he wrote in a letter:

> I composed this opera because I was moved to express in music all that
> seems to cry out for such expression in *Eugene Onegin*. . . . The opera
> *Onegin* will never have a success [at the major houses]: I already feel
> assured of that. . . . I would much prefer to confide it to the theatre of the
> Conservatoire. . . . This is much more suitable to my modest work, which
> I shall not describe as an opera, if it is published. I should like to call it
> "lyrical scenes" or something of that kind. (Letter to S. I. Taniev, January
> 2, 1878, in Tchaikovsky, *Life and Letters*, 255–57)

Moreover, what he seems to have wanted from the Conservatory
students, by contrast with what he thought he would get from singers in the
major theaters, was freshness: "He wanted fresh young voices, performers
untainted by bad habits, a chorus that could act, staging that was simple
and true to the spirit of the 1820s, the sympathetic collaboration of his
friends and of colleagues who really understood what he was trying to
do" (Warrack, program notes, p. 30). That suggests something important
about the way Tchaikovsky imagined his opera: the focus was to be on the
expressive aspects of the story, on its moments of powerful feeling and high
emotional conflict—not, as in Pushkin's poem, on wit, irony, and satire.
Nonetheless, aspects of the social world that Pushkin drew on for his satire
do appear, and they play a significant role in the opera.

The opera opens in the country, in the garden of the Larin estate, where
Madame Larina and Filipyevna, the nurse, are sitting together, thinking
of the past. A couple of visitors, Lensky and Onegin, appear. Lensky is in
love with the younger daughter of the house, Olga; Onegin is his friend.
Onegin is in the country only because he has inherited a small estate from
his uncle; his normal habitat is St. Petersburg and its sophisticated court
society. The two men are of very different temperaments: whereas Lensky
is emotional and impulsive, Onegin is cool, rational, watchful, often bored.
The dreamy and impressionable Tatyana, the elder Larin daughter, falls in
love with him. She writes to him, declaring her love; he speaks to her the
next day, rejecting her kindly but firmly, like an older brother or an uncle,
advising her to take better care, behave less impulsively; she is devastated
but has to accept his decision.

Some months later, there is a ball for Tatyana's name day; Onegin, who
has come with Lensky, is irked by the guests, whom he finds vulgar and
who, in return, disparage him; to annoy Lensky for exposing him to all
this, he flirts with Olga. This has the effect he wants, but it goes too far:
Lensky is provoked enough to challenge Onegin to a duel. The next day,
although neither wants it, the duel takes place, and Lensky is killed. Two

Jennifer Forni as Tatyana in a scene from a 2009 Maryland Opera Studio production of Tchaikovsky's Eugene Onegin. *(Photo by Cory Weaver)*

years later, Onegin is back in St. Petersburg, having gone on his travels to try to exorcise his guilt and overcome his sense of purposelessness; he sees Tatyana at a ball. Tatyana has grown up; she is now a married woman, brilliant, beautiful, and composed. Each is affected by the sight of the other. Days later, after many letters and no answers, Onegin calls to appeal directly to Tatyana. Though she is powerfully moved and in fact admits she still loves Onegin, she will not betray her husband. So this time it is Onegin who is dismissed, sent away with a moral lesson.

Looking at the whole, we can see that the action's development follows a traditional tragic pattern: heightened aspiration, then isolation and defeat. Only here there are two tragic figures, Onegin himself and Tatyana, and their aspirations and disappointments are bound together, though they occur at different times and different ways. In the beginning, Tatyana is a beloved part of her immediate social world, her family, but she is also somewhat apart because of her interest in literature and her imaginative, passionate nature. At the end, although she is a respected part of her world, that same St. Petersburg court society that Onegin frequented, she is still apart. It is her character and her gifts that in both cases distinguish her from the world she is in. But in the end these gifts bring her no joy. She begins with a heart too full, and alone; she ends the same way, her heart at least as full, but this time she is both rejector and rejected, since it is by her own choice that she is left alone in a successful but seemingly passionless marriage. What makes her heroic—and tragic—is her capacity for imaginative feeling, as well as her courage in acting on her feelings. But she is also, in the beginning, gauche and careless; by going behind her mother's back and exposing herself to a man she has known for only a few moments, she takes a big risk. At the end, no longer gauche, she chooses to control her feelings for him, which are no less intense but are indeed now mature and rich, because she refuses to behave dishonorably.

Onegin has also been at odds with his world, but in a more explicit, adversarial way: he is the conventional Romantic hero who sees through everything, who is bored because he can find nothing to attach himself to, nothing that rouses his interest, nothing that seems to him authentic. Of course he has enough money for a comfortable life. His heart is neither empty nor full; rather, it is merely irritated, and in a state of watchful impatience; nothing can measure up to his expectations. At the end, when he does find what he wants, when his heart opens, it is too late. What makes him both heroic and tragic is the capacity for passion that he finds he has in spite of himself, and his courage in acting on this as if he could succeed.

So we have two characters whose capacities and desires are in excess of what their circumstances will allow: this is the classic tragic scenario.

The opera's final scene, where the resolution occurs, is brief, only about fourteen minutes long (depending on the conductor), but it is highly charged with conflict and change; the intense and rapid development of character shown here is remarkable. But to enter it, we need to begin with the scene that directly precedes it, the first scene of Act III.

This opens in a salon adjoining the ballroom of Gremin's (Tatyana's husband's) mansion in St. Petersburg. The guests are dancing a polonaise. It is the first thing we see after the last scene of Act II, which ended with Lensky's body on the ground and the repeated word "ubit" (dead), and since the first person we hear is Onegin, who was responsible for that death, this is a charged entrance (although, apart from the one reference in this aria, Lensky is never referred to again; he has disappeared from the opera). At the beginning of Act III Onegin tells his story:

I zdyes mnye skuchno!	I'm bored here too!
Blyesk i suyeta bolshovo svyeta	The brilliance and whirlwind of society
Ne rassyeyat vyechnoi	Cannot shake my constant
Tomitelnoi toski!	Tiring despair!
Ubiv na poyedinke druga,	I have killed my best friend in a duel,
Dozhiv bez tseli, bez trudov,	I have lived with no ambition, no desire,
Do dvadtsati shesti godov,	To the age of twenty-six
Tomyas bezdyeistviyem dosuga,	Tired by inactivity and idleness, by emptiness;
Bez sluzhbi, bes zheni, bez dyel,	With no purpose, no wife, no occupation,
Sebya zanyat ya ne sumyel!	I have nothing to commit to, to devote myself!
Mnoi ovladyelo bespokoistvo,	I was seized by anxiety,
Okhota k peremyene myest,	And the need to travel,
Vesma muchitelnoye svoistvo,	Quite an unpleasant quality
Nemnogikh dobrovolni kryest!	A cross that few could bear!
Ostavil ya svoyi selyenya	I left my estates in the country,
Lesov i niv uyedinenye,	The solitude of forests and fields,
Gdye okrovavlennaya tyen	Where a bloody ghost
Ko mnye yavlyalas kazhdi dyen!	Accosted me every day!
Ya nachal stranstviya bez tseli	I began to travel, aimlessly,
Dostupni chuvstvu odnomu . . .	Going where my whimsy took me . . .
I shto zh? K neshchastyu moyemu	And what happened? I found, to my misfortune,
I stranstviya mnye nadoyeli!	That travel was boring, too!
Ya vozvratilsa i popal,	I returned and came, like Chatsky,
Kak Chatsky, s korablya na bal!	Straight from a ship to a ball!

Onegin is going to a ball after having been away for two years. He has been gone for two reasons: because he feels guilty about having killed his best friend and in traveling has been trying both to escape and to exorcise his guilt; and because the guilt has increased his habitual state of rootlessness and detachment. As he says, he has come "straight from a ship to a ball"; in effect, he is still on the move, still restless and alone. Though Onegin does not make it easy for us to sympathize with him—we might find him as irritating as he finds himself—we can still with only a little effort recognize a form of despair.

Onegin describes what he wants in negatives; he only says what he does not want: "I zdyes mnye skuchno!" (I'm bored here too!). But a character cannot play not wanting to be in a scene. So the singer has to find a positive before the character steps onstage. That is not hard: a person cannot so strongly *not* want something—as Onegin does *not* want what he sees before him at the ball—without at the same time wanting something better. If Onegin is so antisocial, if he dislikes the presence of this artificial society so much, what motivates his presence at the ball? Clearly he gets something from it. In the rehearsal process it will be interesting to discover what that attraction is. For now it is enough to say that on some level Onegin has both hope and fear: hope that this place will give him or show him something that will engage him enough to allow him to overcome his despair, and fear that it will not. So it is a search for the authentic that is his objective. So far the objective is latent: Onegin does not say to himself directly how much he wants to find what he is looking for. However, we must know from the singer's actions that the hope is nonetheless there. For Onegin it is the old thing, his usual condition of boredom, world-weariness, and self-disgust that is the likely block, as he says at the beginning of his aria. That is a screen that is difficult for anything to penetrate. It could not be gotten through before, when Tatyana first offered herself to him; it would not let him see past her gauche behavior. But balls exist to give opportunities. So Onegin will keep looking around. Almost immediately he sees Tatyana enter. At once the objective that had been hidden—his hope that something could be meaningful for him—flares up. He says:

Uzhel Tatyana? Tochno . . . .nyet! . . .	Can that be Tatyana? Possible . . . no! . . .
Kak! iz glushi stepnikh selyeni?	What? From that village in the steppes?
Ne mozhet bit! Ne mozhet bit!	It's impossible! Impossible!
I kak prosta, kak velichava,	And how simple, how dignified,
Kak nebryezhna! . . .	How perfectly at ease! . . .
Tsaritsei kazhetsa ona!	She bears herself like a queen!

At this point it is mainly his interest that is aroused, not to mention his surprise at seeing her so at ease and composed in this court society; only two years ago she was a provincial, socially awkward young woman. He still has the same objective, to find some relief for his boredom. But now it seems he might succeed, and his intention is focused on finding out what he can about Tatyana. This he achieves by asking his cousin, Prince Gremin, about her.

We see Tatyana at first through the eyes of others and only later through her actions and thoughts. She has come in on the arm of Prince Gremin, so she has a position of importance—she is married to an important man. She is going to greet the other guests. We do not know this from anything she says, only from how she is described by the others and from what she does. The guests say:

Knyaginya Gremina! Smotrite!	Princess Gremina! Look!
Smotrite!	Look!
Kotrorya?	Which one?
Suda vzglyanite!	Over there, look!
Vot ta, shto syela u stola.	The one who sat down at that table.
Bespyechnoi pryelestyu mila!	Her beauty is delightful!

What they say is echoed by what Onegin then says (as above). Evidently she is in this social world but not of it, which is just how she was when we first saw her, in the world of her family but not of it. Her husband—Onegin's cousin—confirms this, telling Onegin before presenting his cousin to his wife:

Sredi lukavikh, malodushnikh,	Among these sly, selfish
Shalnikh, balovannikh detyei,	Foolish, pampered children,
Zlodyeyev i smeshnikh i skuchnikh, ...	These scoundrels both absurd and boring ...
Ona blistayet, kak zvezdza	She shines like a star
Vo mrake nochi, v nyebe chistom, ...	In the night's darkest hour, in a pure, clear sky ...

The difference here is that, far from being the unsophisticated little provincial girl Onegin knew, she is now dignified and composed, enough so that it is the other guests who seek her out to pay their respects. Since she does not seek them, we can say that her objective is simply to appear at the ball as Princess Gremina; she is doing her duty, taking her place in the social world that Gremin inhabits. But there is of course a block, and we discover this as soon as she does: she notices Onegin speaking with her husband and asks who he is. She already knows who he is; why then does she ask the others? Does she do it to cover up her surprise? Or has Onegin changed in appearance so much that she simply does not recognize him at first glance? It has been only two years since they met. He is across a room lit with candles, and so his face may not be easy to make out at a distance. When they tell her it is Onegin, her reaction is strong:

O, Bozhe! pomogi mnye skrit	O God, help me hide
Dushi uzhasnoye volnyenye . . .	The dreadful trembling in my heart! . . .

Seeing him makes it impossible to continue wanting what (we think) she wanted when she came into this room. Why is she so affected? Is she still in love with Onegin? But she is married: hasn't her husband taken Onegin's place in her heart? Does she suddenly remember the shame she felt at Onegin's rejection of her? Does she remember the horror of the argument at her name-day party and the result, Lensky's death? All these are possible. But now she has to act. She has a new objective, and she says what it is: she must hide what she is feeling. And after her husband has brought Onegin over to be presented to her and she has said a few polite words, she has to leave; staying at the ball with Onegin there would be unbearable. The only way she can keep her feelings under control is to leave.

Meanwhile, Onegin himself has suffered a sea change.

Uzhel ta samaya Tatyana,	Can this be the same Tatyana
Kotoroi ya nayedinye,	Whom, when we were together
V glukhoi, dalyokoi storonye,	In the remote countryside,
V blagom pilu nravouchenya,	I, in a splendid moral outburst,
Chital kogda-to nastavlyenya?	Lectured on principles?
Ta dyevochka, kotoroi ya	The same humble girl whom
Prenebregal v smiryennoi dole?	I disdained?
Uzheli to ona bila,	Was that her?
Tak ravnodushna, tak smela?	Who is so poised, so self-possessed?
No shto so mnoi?	But what's the matter with me?
Ya kak vo snye!	I must be in a dream!
Shto shevelnulos v glubinye	What is churning in the depths
Dushi kholodnoi i lenivoi?	Of my cold and lazy heart?
Dosada, suyetnost il vnov,	Irritation, vanity or, once again,
Zabota yunosti—lyubov?	That preoccupation of youth—love?
Uvi, somnyenya nyet, vlyublyon ya,	Alas, there is no doubt I am in love,
Vlyublyon, kak malchik, polni	In love, like a schoolboy, filled with
strasti yunoi.	passion.
Puskai pogibnu ya, no pryezhde	I shall perish, but first
Ya v oslepitelnoi nadyezhde	With blind hope
Vkushu volshebni yad zhelani,	I shall taste the magic poison of desire,
Upyus nesbitochnoi mechtoi!	Sate myself with this impossible dream!
Vezdye, vezdye on predo mnoi,	Everywhere, everywhere I look

| Obraz zhelanni, dorogoi! | I see that beloved, desired image! |
| Vezdye, vezdye, on predo mnoyu! | Wherever I look, I see her! |

The change does not happen at once: Tchaikovsky is careful to show how it develops through memories and questions to a crescendo of erotic rapture. Onegin thinks back, not to his first meeting with Tatyana, of which he had hardly been conscious even at the time, but to his second meeting, when, having read her letter, he not only rejected her but also lectured her on "principles"; now he has only contempt for the way he behaved then. He thinks of the "humble station" she occupied then, as if that could have had something to do with his rejection of her; it probably did, and at this point he is must be aware that it did. He wonders how the poised and self-possessed woman he has just seen can really have been that awkward girl. He senses the stirrings of powerful feelings (the music gains in momentum and is more passionate and insistent) and asks himself what to call them; even when he finally does admit he is in love, he is ironic and self-mocking: "Vlyublyon, kak malchik, polni strasti yunoi" (In love like a boy, a passionate youth). But then the self-mockery suddenly disappears, and he enters a new emotional world where the coordinates are absolute: love and death. The music echoes Tatiana's letter scene. They are similar emotional states. Onegin has become the complete Romantic hero, intoxicated by desire to the point of wishing for death if he could only experience what he dreams of. This is not the kind death we see the Countess wish for in *Figaro*, where it was a despairing response to a painful situation, and a response that was considered and then rejected. It has more in common, perhaps, with Xerxes' desire to pull the world down about his ears because he is not getting what he wants. In fact, he seems to feel it to be a kind of poisonous addiction. So the movement, for Onegin, is from too little feeling, awareness, and participation to what he might see as too much. Is this the redemptive, absorbing passion he has always sought? Perhaps. But it is risky, especially for a man who has kept himself as apart as Onegin has. Which is perhaps why he is also aware, in the midst of all his hyperbole, of its dangers: he realizes, and eagerly accepts, that to surrender to this passion invites destruction: "Puskai pogibnu ya" (Let me perish).

Why are these feelings sweeping over him? Is it just because Tatyana, as a married woman, is now unattainable? Is it because she seems to be able to walk away from him with ease, treating him the way he had treated earlier her in the country? Is it because she is no longer a gauche and overeager girl, but a mature, beautiful, and self-possessed woman? Is it because everyone else at the ball is enraptured by her? Whatever the reason, it is clear that

Onegin has found exactly what he was looking for—in fact, what he was likely looking for at the beginning of the opera when he let his friend Lensky draw him out to pay a visit in the country: something or someone authentic. Whatever the reason, he now has a new and overwhelming objective: to win her.

As the second scene opens we learn Tatyana's new objective. She is in a room in her husband's house in St. Petersburg. The musical introduction to this last scene is in effect a description of Tatyana's life from the time she encountered Onegin to the present, at which point she enters. It starts calmly, but has movement; like Onegin's aria it mounts to a crescendo. It begins with the marking *moderato* but then becomes agitated; the tempo increases (*stringendo*), and the marking changes to *più mosso*. So when Tatyana finally enters, she enters in the state to which the music has taken her—passionate, fearful, and full of conflict. She is holding a letter, evidently from Onegin, perhaps the latest of many. We can imagine what the letters contain: a new Onegin is revealed, an Onegin who is the lover she had once so intensely wished him to be. The effects on her of seeing him at the ball and then receiving his avowals have been powerful: she has had to realize she has never stopped loving him, even though because of her marriage and the passage of time she has forced him from her mind.

O! Kak mnye tyazhelo!	Oh, how distressed I am!
Opyat Onegin stal na puti moyom,	Once more Onegin has crossed my path
Kak prizrak besposhchadni!	Like a relentless apparition!
On vzorom ognennim	His burning glance
Mnye dushu vozmutil,	Has troubled my heart
On strast zaglokhshuyu kak zhivo voskresil	And reawakened my dormant passion
Kak budto snova dyevochkoi ya stalaso	So that I feel like a young girl again
Kak budto s nim menya nishto ne razluchalo!	And as if nothing had ever parted us!

The image of Onegin as a "prizrak besposhchadni" (relentless apparition) is key; it is as if Onegin is some kind of demon lover she has always known in the depths of her unconscious, half expected, both feared and desired. In fact, she had said as much in her letter to him two years before:

Kto ti: moi angel li khranitel,	Who are you? My guardian angel,
Ili kovarni iskusitel?	or a wily tempter?

It is odd and worth noting that, although in different ways, each imagines the other or his or her feelings for the other as being malign and destructive. And they are not wrong: their feelings for each other will harm them. Moreover, what they feel for each other has already begun to affect those around them: in the ball scene, Prince Gremin's sang his aria in praise of married love directly after Tatyana's passionate outburst (which he did not hear) on seeing Onegin; at once, without knowing it, he has become a victim of their feelings for each other.

As for Tatyana, she knows that her feelings for Onegin are quite different from her feelings for her husband, and that terrifies her. When she comes into this room, now, it is as if she is trying to get away from something. Or, perhaps, to get *to* something. She ends with the image of herself as a young girl again and the thought that nothing had ever parted them. She is partly lost in wishfulness, a wishfulness that goes back to her state of mind when she was writing her letter: in reality, she and Onegin had never been "together," so there never was any relationship from which to part, except in her own imagination. But now the object of her fancy has appeared again; in a few moments he will appear in this room. She must have allowed this. People in these social circles do not just walk in off the street—servants have orders to let some in and keep others out—so she must be expecting Onegin, be prepared for him, even. That means she is not trying to get away from anything; rather, she intends this meeting to take place. Why? Because she knows she has to deal with him, and with her own feelings for him. Perhaps she is allowing herself to feel the power of these feelings as a preparation for dealing with them? Her objective, then, must be to cope with what is before her: the return of the man she had loved and the reawakening of her feelings for him.

In playing the scene, she has some choices to make. She can play it wanting Onegin but denying that she does. She can play it trying to figure out how to go away with him. She can play the scene hating him—for reappearing and reanimating all the feelings she had thought were buried. She can play the scene hating herself—for being still so vulnerable to him. Or, as she plays the scene, all these ideas can be explored.

The music for Onegin's entrance is grand: full of fury, desperation, and desire. It is passionate and wild; it leads to his entry, just as Tatyana's entrance music did, and prepares us for what to expect. But for all that, it is not he who has the first words; all he does is hurl himself to his knees before her. It is Tatyana who speaks first, and when she does, her music is calm and measured, though also full of desire:

Dovolno, vstante, ya dolzhna   Enough, get up, I must
Vam obyasnitsa otkrovyenno.   Talk to you frankly.

Onegin, pomnite l tot chas	Onegin, do you remember that time
Kogda v sadu, v allyeye nas	When, on the garden path,
Sudba svela i tak smiryenno	Fate brought us together and I listened
Urok vash vislushala ya?	Meekly to your lecture?

The dynamics of power at this moment are striking: it is she who is in command; it is she who stops him from speaking, who gets him up off his knees; and it is she who sets the topic. Why does she choose this particular topic, making them both think back to the scene in her garden when he rejected her? Just before he appeared, she had remembered the past quite differently; but now there are other things on her mind. What she is recalling—for them both—is the painful aspects of that scene in the past. Why? To remember it must be unpleasant, and perhaps that will make her angry—at Onegin, naturally, but also at herself. Then what is her intention here? Perhaps, by recalling his rejection of her, she is forcing them both to acknowledge a reality: the way she behaved then, as suppliant; the way he behaved, as rejector. She says she "listened . . . meekly to your lecture." That was then; now she wants it to be clear that she will not play that role here, that in fact the roles are reversed. Is she asserting this to convince him or herself? Or both?

His response is to beg:

O, szhaltes, szhaltes nado mnoyu!	O spare me, have pity!
Ya tak oshibsa, ya tak	I was so mistaken; I have been cruelly
nakazan!	punished.

He is on the defensive, his initiative taken away; he cannot assert what he wants to assert. How does she react? Is she moved? Does she reach out her hand to him? Is she in tears? She can be; she does not have to be. Or is she impatient? Evidently she has more to say. She motions to him to be quiet, to not interrupt her. There are six bars with a *ritardando* as she collects herself. Perhaps her tactic of taking control has been too successful: could seeing Onegin as a suppliant lover have suppressed her anger at him? She needs the brief pause. Then her aria begins; the music is *andantino* and *piano*, calm and rational; it has movement, but movement that is always under control.

Onegin! Ya togda molozhe,	Onegin, I was younger then,
Ya luchshe, kazhetsa, bila!	And a better person!
I ya lyubila vas, no shto zhe	And I loved you, but what, then
Shto v vashem syerdtse ya nashla,	What response did I find
Kakoi otvyet? Odnu surovst!	In your heart? Only severity!

Ne pravda l, vam bila ne novost
Smiryennoi dyevochki
   lyubov?
I ninch . . . Bozhe, stinet
   krov,
Kak tolko vspomnyu vzglyad
   etu propoved!
No vas ya ne vinyu . . .
V tot strashni chas
Vi postupili blagorodno
Vi bili pravi predo mnoi,
Togda, ne pravda li, v pustine,
Vdali ot suyetnoi
   molvi,
Ya vam ne nravilas; shto zh nine
Menya preslyeduyete vi?
Zachem u vas ya na primyete?
Ne potomu l, shto v visshem svyete
Tepyer yavlyatsa ya dolzhna,
Shto ya bogata i znatna,
Shto muzh v srazhenyakh
   izuvyechen,
Shto nas za to laskayet
   dvor?
Ne potomu l, shto moi pozor
Tepyer bi vsyemi bil zamyechen
I mog bi v obshchestve prinyest
Vam soblaznitelnuyu chest?

Am I not right in thinking that
A simple young girl's love was nothing
   new to you?
Even now . . . dear God, my blood runs
   cold
Whenever I recall that icy look, that I
   sermon!
But I do not blame you . . .
In that awful moment
You behaved honorably,
You acted correctly toward me.
Isn't it true, at the time,
In the wilderness, away from the vain
   gossip,
You didn't find me attractive? Why, then,
Do you pursue me now?
Why am I the object of such attentions?
Could it be because I now
Appear in the highest circles,
Because I am rich and noble,
Because my husband is a veteran
   of battles,
Because of this we are favored by
   the court?
Could it not be that my disgrace
Would now be generally known
And could bring you, in society
A seductive honor?

The aria is so carefully structured that it seems unlikely that Tatyana would not have thought hard about this meeting, even about how to conduct it. She presents a series of arguments that are linked to specific events, moving in time from the past to the present. Her aim is to present him with a picture of himself—and of herself—then and now, and to use these images to explain his motivation. This in turn will make it easy for her to reject him. But as the dramatic dynamic markings show, her argument is highly charged. It is not as if she has memorized a speech; at every point she is tentatively finding her way. She begins with what she was two years before, what she did then, and what he did in response; her love for him then was the love of "a simple young girl," and perhaps, she says, he'd had other affairs with simple young girls. She calls his behavior to her severe, but also says he behaved "honorably" and "acted correctly" toward her. What is she doing? It seems that she is not only arranging her own thoughts about these events, including reexperiencing her horror at the look on his face and at his sermon ("my blood runs cold"), but also presenting him with a simple and unflattering truth: that because he was more experienced than she and much more polished, it was not difficult for him to behave honorably. In other words, his behavior was more self-interested than honorable; he just did not find her attractive enough to act dishonorably. It follows that, having not found her attractive then, "in the back of beyond," for him to pursue her now can only mean that he is interested in her only because of her position. What he wants, she claims, is to win her away from her husband and thereby to make a sexual conquest and gain the reputation of a seducer. The anger in these words is palpable; perhaps she will show it; perhaps not; in any case, the effect on Onegin will be powerful. To the extent that she is feeling her way through these arguments, they must be painful for her: they are an intense and complex mixture of anger, regret, horror, desire, anger again, perhaps contempt, again regret. The whole point is for her to put him in his place—and by doing that to put her own feelings in their place.

His response is tempestuous.

Akh! O Bozhe! Uzhel,	Oh! My God!
Uzhel v molbye moyei smiryennoi	Is it possible that in my humble pleading
Uvidit vash kholodni vzor	Your icy look sees nothing
Zatyeyi khitrosti prezryennoi?	But a deception of despicable cunning?
Menya terzayet vash ukor!	Your reproach torments me!
Kogda b vi znali, kak uzhasno	If you only knew how terrible
Tomitsa zhazhdoyu lyubvi,	To have this thirst for love,
Pilat i razumom vsyechasno	To have to constantly check
Smiryat volnyenye v kkrovi,	The passionate fever in my blood,
Zhelat obnyat u vas kolyeni	To want to clasp your knees
I, zaridav u vashikh nog,	And, weeping at your feet,
Islit molbi, priznanya, pyeni,	Pour out entreaties, confessions, complaints,
Vsyo, vsyo shto virazit bi mog!	All, all that words can express!

There is a fermata on the word "Bozhe" (My God), as if Onegin can hardly believe what he has heard. He is astonished at her accusation. The fermata lets him gather his thoughts—although, as they emerge, they turn out not to be very ordered. But under the circumstances, that hardly matters: in the end, they will have an effect. He cries, "Kogda b vi znali, kak uzhasno tomitsa zhazhdoyu lyubvi" (If you only knew how terrible to have this thirst for love). But of course she knows that very well: it is exactly what she experienced when she wrote her letter to him two years ago and then suffered his rejection. Onegin is not presenting the well-prepared ideas she has just given him; rather, they come direct from his heart, with great intensity, as if he had passed beyond the state of merely being in love. Instead, what he shows is need: raw, authentic, and profound.

Tatyana is able to respond Onegin's need exactly as he wants: "Ya plachu!" (I'm weeping!), she cries. Why can she respond this way, at this point? Partly because she is seeing the lover she had always hoped Onegin would be, not cold and superior, but vulnerable and passionate. Therefore she can move past her feelings of anger to sympathy; she feels *with* him. To which he in turn responds:

Plachte, eti slyozi	Weep, those tears are dearer
Dorozhe vsyekh sokrovishch mira!	Than all the treasures in the world!

His music is calm, almost tranquil: it seems he has gotten what he wants, gotten her past her angry defenses, won her again. And this she seems to confirm:

Akh! shchastye bilo tak vozmozhno,	Ah! Happiness was within our reach,
Tak blizko! Tak blizko!	So close! So close!

They repeat the refrain, together. The music is rich—calm and hopeful, full of feeling. Is she yielding to Onegin? It is clear in the music that her desire is to go with him, that that is her real objective. But then the music changes: the tempo is the same, but the character and meter change.

No sudba moy uzh reshena,	But my fate has already been decided,
i bezvozratno!	and irrevocably!
Ya vishla zamuzh, vi dolzhni,	I am married; you must,
Y vas proshu menya ostavit!	I beg you, leave me!

She is returning to her former position, to holding back—not angry, as she was before, but rather determined. She has acquired an ally: fate. Her world is beyond choice and therefore beyond change. What they just now sang together—"Tak blizko!" (So close!)—meant to each of them something different. To him, it meant hope, looking ahead; but to her, it can only mean the present—obligation, honor, and regret. Her objective has not changed. In fact, it is now strengthened: because she has allowed herself to feel and express her feelings of love, she knows clearly what she has to overcome. Her marriage is irrevocable; therefore he must leave.

Her response throws Onegin into despair:

Ostavit! Ostavit! Kak!	Leave you? Leave you! What!
. . . vas ostavit?	. . . Leave you?

Nyet! Nyet!	No! No!
Pominutno videt vas,	To see you always,
Povsyudu slyedovat za vami,	To dog your footsteps, to follow
Ulibku ust, dvizhenye, vzglyad	Your every smile, movement, and glance
Lovit vlyublyonnimi glazami,	With admiring eyes,
Vnimat vam dolgo, ponimat	To listen to you for hours, to understand
Dushoi vsyo vashe sovershenstvo,	In my very being all your perfection,
Pred vami v strastnikh mukakh zamirat,	To faint before you in passionate torment,
Blednyet i gasnut: vot blazhenstvo	Turn pale and die: this is bliss,
Vot odna mechta moya, odno blazhenstvo!	This is my only dream, my only happiness!

The language he uses is a measure of his desperation. The way he visualizes himself with her is the complete antithesis of anything we have seen of him in the past. The images of him following her hour by hour, watching every movement, hanging on her every word, swooning before her—these are images of almost childlike dependency, not so much of love. They are rhetorical tactics, of course—devices that he hopes will move her. He is relentless, doing whatever he can think of to rouse her feelings, shake her resolution. But his entreaties also reveal his state. The crescendo comes on the image of death that he seems to imagine will come from their union: "Pred vami v strastnikh, mukakh zamirat, Blednyet i gasnut" (To faint before you in passionate torment, turn pale and die). Is it his thought that together in ecstasy they would die—the quintessentially Romantic thought, that lovers can unite only in death? Is there an implied threat here—that if Tatyana will not come with him, he will die? Whatever the case, this is not fair; in ordinary discourse we would quickly see through it and turn away. But ordinary discourse is not what's being presented here; like Tatyana, we are moved.

But perhaps, like her, we are also a little frightened: she draws away, trying to find words that will recall him to his moral sense:

Onegin, v vashem syerdtse yest	Onegin, in your heart there is
I gordost, i pryamaya chest!	Both pride and honor!

But she is also fighting herself: the music is marked *andante molto mosso, forte, con anima*; it shows how much she wants to go with him. Perhaps he hears this too, for he does not hold back: "Ya ne mogu ostavit vas!" (I cannot leave you!). Finally it is her turn to beg: "Ya vas proshu menya ostavit" (I beg you to leave me). What is her state of mind? Is she ready once again to give in? Has he won her? The power seems to have shifted to him. Her music shows this; it is agitated, *più mosso*: "Zachem skrivat, zachem lukavit?" (Why hide it, why pretend?). There's another change; the music is marked *forte*, as if she is defying her fate: "Akh! Ya vas lyublyu!" (Ah! I love you!). She may fall into his arms; she may just reach out for him. Whatever her choice is, Onegin exults:

Shto slishu ya?	What am I hearing?
Kakoye slovo ti skazala!	What was that word you spoke?
O, radost! zhizn moya!	O joy! O, my life!
Ti pryezhneyu Tatyanoi stala!	You are again the Tatyana of my former days!

But he speaks too soon. She can see how she is behaving, and, hearing what he says, she comes in effect to consciousness again. There is a series of *forte* chords and the marking *molto più vivo*. She will not give in, not betray her marriage, not challenge her fate; she will fulfill her own moral code. Her decision is irrevocable:

Nyet! Nyet!	No! No!
Proshlovo ne vorotit!	You cannot bring back the past!
Ya otdana tepyer drugomu,	I am another's now,
Moya sudba uzh reshena,	My fate is already decided,
Ya budu vyek yemu verna.	I shall always be true to him.

Here the choices are strong. She can hate herself, Onegin, even Gremin; at the same time, she is nearly overcome with love for Onegin. This is an almost paralyzing conflict, and it must be intolerable for her. The music is marked *forte, molto più vivo*. It's followed by eight bars of music marked only *allegro moderato*. Why? She should leave, but she does not. Why not? Because she knows that when she does it will be the last she will ever see of Onegin. This is not a moment for frailty and swooning. In fact, it is for her the climax of the opera—of her life—the point of no return. So can she not relish her love, even if only for a moment?

The music tells Onegin to make his case even more strongly. He summons the best arguments he can:

O, ne goni, menya ti lyubish!	Oh, do not drive me away; you love me!
I ne ostavlyu ya tebya	And I will not leave you!
Ti zhizn svoyu naprasno sgubish!	You will ruin your life for nothing!
To volya nyeba: ti moya!	This is the will of Heaven: you are mine!
Vsya zhizn tvoya bila zalogom	All your life has been a vow
Soyedinyeniya so mnoi!	Of our union!
I znai: tebye ya poslan Bogom,	And be assured, I was sent to you by God,
Do groba ya khranitel tvoi!	I am your protector to the grave!

Ne mozhesh ti menya otrinut,
Ti dlya menya dolzhna pokinut
Postili dom, i shumni
   svyet—
Tebye drugoi dorogi nyet!

You cannot refuse me,
For me you must forsake
This hateful house, the shrieks of
   society—
You have no choice!

In this we see distortion, willfulness. It is in the nature of the debate that this be so—Onegin is fighting for his life. Against Tatyana's arguments about fate he proposes a different fate: that they have always been meant for each other, from the beginning; that he has been sent to her by God. Against her attempt to be moral he holds up his own experience, that society is corrupt. That is always how he has presented himself, from Act I—as the kind of person who sees through the emptiness and hypocrisy of social conventions; it was how he behaved when he entered the side room at the ball at the beginning of the act. (Ironically, it is also what Prince Gremin talks about when he is describing why he loves his wife.) But when he says the last line, "Tebye drugoi dorogi nyet!" (You have no choice!), he makes a mistake. Being told that she has no choice reminds Tatyana that she has in fact made her choice. At once she rises to her feet, resolved: "Onegin, ya tverda ostanus" (Onegin, I shall remain firm). And he knows he has lost. From then until the end are only recapitulation and finality. They sing together (except for his first and her last lines), but at the same time they are ineluctably apart:

ONEGIN
. . . Ti dlya menya . . .
. . . dolzhn pokinut vsyo, vsyo—
Postili dom i shumni svyet!
Tebye drugoi dorogi nyet!
O, ne goni menya, molyu!
Ti lyubish menya; ti zhizn svoyu
Naprasno sgubish!
Ti moya, navyek moya!

ONEGIN
. . . For me . . .
. . . you must forsake all, all—
Hateful house and social babble!
You have no choice!
Oh, do not drive me from you,
I beg you! You love me; you will destroy
Your life for nothing!
You are mine, mine for ever!

TATYANA
. . . Nyet, klyatvi pomnit ya . . .
   dolzhna!
Gluboko v syerditse proninkayet,
Yevo otchayanni priziv,
No, pil prestupni podaviv,
Dolg chesti surovi, svyashchenni
Chuvstvo pobezhdayet!
Ya udalyayus!

TATYANA
No, I must keep my
   vows!
Deep in my heart his desperate appeal
Demands an answering chord,
But I must stifle the sinful flame,
And honor's harsh and sacred duty
Will triumph over the passion!
I'm leaving you!

Both passages show their characters' needs—but not, in Tatyana's case, her desire. Or, at least, not desire to which she yields. The music is sensuous but rapid. After a few more brief exchanges, she does leave, and he is entirely alone. His response to this finality is surprising:

Pozor! . . . Toska!	Ignominy! . . . Anguish!
O zhalki, zhrebi moi!	Oh, my pitiable fate!

"Ignominy"? Why that word, when there might be so many others? How is he seeing himself at this moment, when he has lost everything he had ever wanted? Not as a tragic person, forever alone; not as someone who has lost his love. Rather, as a fool, as he might be seen by others—from the outside, not from within. Why?

Well, this may be a question for the green room or the bar. For our purposes, we should simply note again the classic tragic behavior: how fiercely both characters fight for what they desire. Right to the end, the logic of the form dictates this rage for life. The opera ends not because the lives of Tatyana and Onegin are over, any more than their love is over, but because—in the world of that love—there is nowhere else to go. A limit has been reached.

Perhaps that helps us understand why Onegin's first reaction is "Pozor!" (Ignominy!). It is as if a lifelong fear has come true, a fear that has always crept along beside his desire: not that he will be alone, not that he will lose a woman he loves, but that he will be thought ridiculous. Now it is the dismisser who has been dismissed. What he seems to regret—what he seems to say he regrets—is the loss of his persona, his social identity, his guise. It is not the loss of his heart's desire. His tragedy is unlike Tatyana's. What she will hear, from now on, is only her husband's voice, not the voice of her beloved; what Onegin will hear, he knows, is the mocking laughter of people he despises.

CONCLUSION

N OT LONG AGO I met a friend who had seen a performance of a new opera I had directed. He congratulated me, saying he and his wife had spent several hours discussing the production. His wife had liked it, but not he; she had connected to it instantly, while he had struggled and not been able to find a way in. Still, they had talked—about the text, about the music, about the themes of the piece—trying to understand what it was that had spoken to one but not to the other. I found this all quite encouraging.

Often people find themselves stimulated to talk this way about plays they have seen. But since opera is by nature a feeling medium—depending on the human voice in song—talk about it tends to focus on different things: the tenor's high *C*, the soprano's lovely *pianissimo*, the way the show was lit, the look, the feel. Comparisons are made: between singers one has heard, productions one has seen, conductors. It is all art chat: at its best, about elements of craft; at its worst, one-upmanship. Usually themes are not discussed, nor why a character behaved the way he did, nor the significance of a piece of staging, nor what the composer might have had in mind by the way he set the ensemble at the end.

However, if the world created by the singers is "real" enough, perhaps it is possible to get beyond this and into something more substantial?

Opera is an artificial event, but artificial events do not negate the reality of the relationships or the characters' actions. "Real" in the performing arts does not mean a naturalistic representation of life. It means creating a world for the particular opera and remaining consistent within that particular world. That is the essence of storytelling. The stories we read to our children are consistent in the world they create; there are no contradictions, and they are believed because we, and our children, accept that world as reality. Opera is storytelling, whether it be of an Egyptian slave or bohemian Paris or dying courtesans. As long as the world in which the opera is clothed is consistent, we can accept it. The fact that an opera is sung does not imply that it is false. When singers create roles, they are doing so with the most personal of all musical instruments. Singing as a means of communication is itself artificial, but that does not make it less true.

It has been the argument of this book that what "real" means for the performance of opera comes from the recognition that opera is a theatrical event; it does not take place in a concert hall or on a CD. It is performed in three dimensions. Certain elements of craft can make such a performance powerful, and one of the most important of these is acting. If the people we see on an opera stage are not only singing wonderfully but also acting—doing their best to *be* the characters whose voices they are using—then the power that is already there in the music and the words can be unleashed, and the experience we in the audience will have can be magnificent.

It is the filled, enacted human voice that takes us inside an opera. Or, as in the case of my friend who found he could not enter a particular production, that leaves questions in the air, to be discussed, engaged with. And that, to my mind, is the great thing an art can do: to draw us on, engage us, take us somewhere new.

ACKNOWLEDGMENTS

I N A PROJECT THAT HAS GROWN over the years, many debts accrue. In fact, they go back far beyond the time when the project began.

Two people long ago influenced the way I think about the theater. The first was Robert Gill. He was a director, acting teacher, and producer of genius at the University of Toronto. He put up with me as a student actor—he knew I did not really want to be an actor—and spent many hours teaching me principles of directing. He was devoted to the theater, and very generous with anyone whom he thought took it seriously. The second, the person who taught me most about directing opera, Herman Geiger-Torel, who, from 1956 to 1976 was the first artistic director of what is now the Canadian Opera Company. He patiently showed me the way things were traditionally done and then gave me the freedom to depart from those traditions and explore new ideas and approaches to opera.

As we all do in the arts, I have learned from watching, from reading, and from working with a number of gifted and talented people. I have watched acting teachers in their studios, like Stella Adler and Uta Hagen; in the late 1950s I watched rehearsals at the Berliner Ensemble. I've read some influential theorists, especially Stanislavsky, Uta Hagen and Peter Brook. And I've learned from my colleagues at the Maryland Opera Studio, at the University of Maryland in College Park.

I have been fortunate to have such talented, inventive and generous professionals to work with. I am the recipient of their expertise. I am also grateful to the many singers I have had the pleasure and privilege of teaching. They undoubtedly taught me much more than I taught them. I am indebted to Garnett Bruce, Dominic Cossa, Miah Im, Erie Mills, Nick Olcott, and Charley Rutherford who read the manuscript and were more than generous in sharing their valuable and insightful comments.

Especially to be thanked are Geraldine Sherman, Robert Fulford, and Mark Strand; each read very early drafts of the manuscript and encouraged me to continue, as did Beverely Slopen, my literary agent, whose patience I greatly appreciated. I would also thank Jessica Burr, my editor, and Barbara Norton, my copy editor, whose wise advice certainly improved the manuscript. And to those individuals whom I have not mentioned but who offered comments and suggestions, my deepest gratitude. As always, errors, omissions, and other deficiencies are my own.

GLOSSARY

accompagnato: accompanied by the orchestra, rather than by the continuo; see also *secco*

adagio: at ease; play slowly

allegretto: a little lively; moderately fast

allegretto vivace: moderately quick

allegrissimo: very fast, though slower than *presto*

allegro: cheerful or brisk; but commonly interpreted as lively, fast

alto: lit., high; to the second-highest of the standard four voice ranges, taken in all-male ensembles by men but in mixed groups by women; see also *soprano*, *tenor*, and *bass*; *contralto*

andante: walking pace; i.e., at a moderate tempo

andante molto mosso, forte, con anima: at a walking pace, but more roughly, strongly, and animatedly

andantino: an ambiguous term meaning either a little faster or a little slower, usually the former

animato: animated, lively

a piacere: at pleasure; at the singer's discretion

appassionato: passionately

aria: lit., air; a formally constructed air or song in an opera

arietta: a short *aria*

arioso: airy, or like an air (melody); in the manner of an aria; airy, breezy

a tempo: in time; i.e., the performer should return to the main tempo of the piece (after an *accelerando* or *ritardando*, etc.); also may be found in combination with other terms such as *a tempo giusto* (in strict time) or *a tempo di menuetto* (at the speed of a minuet)

attacca: attack, go on; i.e., at the end of a movement, a direction to begin ("attack") the next movement immediately, without a gap or pause

bar: see *measure*

bar line: in musical notation, a vertical line drawn through the staff that marks off one group of beats from another; see also *measure bass*: (1) the lowest of the standard four voice ranges; see also *soprano*, *alto*, and *tenor*; (2) the lowest melodic line in a musical composition, often thought of as defining and supporting the *harmony*; (3) short term for double bass (musical instrument)

basso continuo: continuous bass; i.e., a bass part played continuously throughout a piece to give harmonic structure, used especially in the Baroque period

beat: in music, a regular rhythmical pattern; in drama, a unit of action that is complete in itself

brio: vigor; usually seen in the phrase *con brio*

cadence: a sequence of chords that provides musical punctuation at the end of a phrase

cadenza: form of virtuoso embellishment; based originally on an extended final cadence, it was originally improvised by the performer, though in the nineteenth century cadenzas came to be written out by composers

cantabile, *cantando*: in a lyric style

capo: head; i.e., the beginning (of a movement)

cesura, **(Latin)** *caesura*: break, stop; i.e., a complete break in sound (sometimes called "railroad tracks" in reference to their notation as a pair of parallel lines)

chord: the simultaneous sounding of two or more notes in harmony

crescendo: growing, becoming louder; gradually increasing in volume

coda: tail; i.e., a closing section appended to a movement

col, colla: with the (*col* before a masculine noun, *colla* before a feminine noun); see, e.g., *colla voce*

colla voce: with the voice; as an instruction in a choral or opera score or orchestral part, it instructs the conductor or orchestral musician to follow the rhythm and tempo of a solo singer (usually for a short passage)

coloratura: lit., coloration; i.e., elaborate ornamentation of a vocal line; also, a type of soprano voice well suited to such elaboration

con amore, (Spanish and sometimes Italian) *con amor*: with love; tenderly

con anima: with feeling

con brio: with spirit, with vigor

con dolore: with sadness

con forza: with force

con (gran, molto) espressione: with (great, much) expression

con moto: with motion

contralto: the lowest range of the female voice, usually extending from about the F below middle C to the D an octave and a step above it; see also *alto*

crescendo: growing; i.e., progressively louder; see also *diminuendo da capo*: from the head; i.e., from the beginning; see *capo*

da capo aria: an aria in three sections, of which the third is an improvised and usually ornamented repetition of the first; most common in the late Baroque period

decrescendo, decresc.: see *diminuendo, dim.*

diminuendo, dim.: dwindling; i.e., with gradually decreasing volume

discovery: a character's realization that an aspect of the opera's action will require his or her objective or intention to change

dolcissimo: very sweetly

doloroso: sorrowfully, plaintively

doppio movimento: twice as fast

dolce: softly, sweetly

dynamics: the relative volume levels in the execution of a piece of music. Dynamics in a piece should be interpreted relative to the other dynamics in the same piece. For example, *pp* should be executed as softly as possible, but if *ppp* is found later in the piece, the *pp* should be louder than *ppp*. The more *p*s or *f*s are written, the softer or louder the composer wants the musician to play or sing

falsetto: technique used by male voices to produce pitches above the usual bass or tenor range

fermata: musical notation indicating that a particular note or rest should be held longer than its value would suggest, at the performer's or conductor's discretion, for dramatic effect

flat: a symbol (♭) that, when printed before a note, lowers its pitch by a semitone.

forte, f: strong; i.e., to be played or sung loudly

fortepiano, fp: loud, then immediately soft; see *dynamics*

fortissimo, ff: very loud, powerful; see also *dynamics*

fortississimo, fff: as loud as possible; see also *dynamics*

forza: musical force

forzando, fz: see *sforzando*

fuoco: fire; *con fuoco*, with fire

G.P.: grand pause; indicates to the performers that the entire ensemble has a rest of indeterminate length, often as a dramatic effect during a loud section

grandioso: grandly

grave: slowly and seriously

grazioso: gracefully

improvvisato: improvised, or as if improvised

intention: what an actor or singer wants at any given moment in a scene; see also *objective*

introduction: the opening section of a piece of music

lacrimoso: tearfully; i.e., sadly

largamente: broadly, slowly; see also *largo*

larghetto: slowly, though not as slowly as *largo*

largo: very slowly, so as to give an sense of spaciousness; large, wide, broad *legato*: joined; i.e., smoothly, in a connected manner; see also *articulation*

leggiero, *leggermente*: lightly, delicately

lento: slowly

l'istesso: see *lo stesso*

lo stesso, or, commonly but ungrammatically, *l'istesso*: the same; applied to the manner of articulation, tempo, etc.

lunga pausa: break, pause; lit., a long stop

ma non troppo: but not too much

madrigal: a form of part-song for three to eight voices, popular in the Renaissance and early Baroque periods

marcia: a march; *alla marcia*, in the manner of a march

melisma: the technique of singing several pitches on a single syllable

measure: the period of a musical piece encompassing a complete cycle of the time signature; e.g., in 4/4 time, a measure has four quarter-note beats

meno: less; see, e.g., *meno mosso*, under *mosso*

meter: the pattern of a musical piece's rhythm of strong and weak beats

mezza voce: half voice; i.e., with subdued or moderated volume

mezzo: half; see, e.g., *mezzo forte*, *mf*

mezzo forte, *mf*: half loudly; i.e., moderately loudly; see also *dynamics*

mezzo piano, *mp*: half softly; i.e., moderately softly; see also *dynamics*

mezzo-soprano: a female singer with a range usually extending from the A below middle C to the F an eleventh above middle C. Mezzo-sopranos generally have a darker vocal tone than sopranos, and their vocal range is between those of a *soprano* and an *alto*

moderato: moderate; often combined with other terms, usually relating to tempo, e.g., *allegro moderato*

molto: very

mosso: moved, moving; used with a preceding *più* or *meno* (which see) for faster or slower, respectively

moto: motion; usually seen in the phrase *con moto*, with motion or quickly

moderato: moderate, tempered, mild; moderate speed; can be used with other terms, e.g., *allegro moderato*, moderately fast

molto più vivo: much more lively

objective: what an actor or singer wants upon entering a scene

opera seria: a form of serious Italian opera popular from the early eighteenth century to around 1770; it came to be governed by strict rules regarding subject and characterization

parlando, *parlante*: speechlike; enunciated

pastorale: in a pastoral style; i.e., peaceful and simple

pausa: rest

pianissimo, *pp*: very gently; i.e., played very softly, even softer than *piano* see also *pianissississimo*, *ppp*: very, very gently; i.e., played as softly as possible

piano, *p*: gently; i.e., played or sung softly; see *dynamics*

piano-vocal score: a score of an opera, cantata, or other large work for voice(s) and orchestra in which the vocal parts are written out in full but the accompaniment is reduced to two staves and adapted for playing on piano

più: more; see, e.g., *mosso*

poco: a little; e.g., *poco più allegro*, a little faster

poco a poco: little by little

portamento: carrying; sliding in pitch from one note to another, usually pausing just above or below the final pitch, then sliding quickly to that pitch.

prestissimo: extremely fast; as quickly as possible

presto: very quickly

prima volta: the first time; e.g., *prima volta senza accompagnamento*, the first time without accompaniment

primo (masc.), *prima* (fem.): first

piano, *p*: gently; i.e., to be played softly

pianissimo, *pp*, *double piano*: very gently; i.e., to be played very softly

più mosso: more moved, more agitated; i.e., to be played faster

rallentando, *rall.*: broadening of the tempo; progressively slower; see also *ritardando*

rallentando un poco: slowing down a little; i.e., to be played gradually a bit more slowly

rapido: fast

recitative: a style of delivery for the solo voice that is close to ordinary speech; usually accompanied by a harpsichord (*recitativo secco*), sometimes by more instruments (*recitativo accompagnato*); used to move the action ahead

ritardando, *ritard.*, *rit.*: slowing down, decelerating; see also *accelerando*

ritenuto, *riten.*, *rit.*: suddenly slower, held back; usually more so but more temporarily than *ritardando*; may, unlike *ritardando*, apply to a single note

ritornello: a short instrumental passage; also, a recurring passage for orchestra in the first or final movement of a solo concerto or aria, or a work for chorus

rondo: a musical form in which a certain section returns repeatedly, interspersed with other sections: ABACA is a typical *rondo* structure

rubato: robbed; in music, refers to *tempo rubato* (lit., robbed time), i.e., a flexible tempo applied for expressive effect to notes within a musical phrase that may

introduce or punctuate an aria

scherzando, scherzoso: playfully

scherzo: joking; a light, playful musical form, originally and usually in fast triple *meter*, often replacing the minuet in the later Classical period and the Romantic period in symphonies, sonatas, string quartets and the like; in the nineteenth century some scherzi were independent movements for piano or another instrument

secco: dry; accompanied by continuo; see also *accompagnato*

segno: sign; usually seen in the phrase *dal segno*, from the sign, i.e., returning to the point marked by D.S. or 𝄋

segue: carry on to the next section without a pause

sforzando, sfz: made loud; i.e., a sudden strong accent

sharp: a symbol (#) that, when printed before a note, raises its pitch by a semitone

sinfonia: symphony; in seventeenth- and eighteenth-century opera, an instrumental passage often used as an introduction

solo (sing.), *soli* (pl.): alone; i.e., executed by a single instrument or voice. The instruction *soli* requires more than one player or singer

soprano: the highest of the standard four voice ranges, generally extending from about middle C upward as high, in opera, as the F three and a half octaves above; see also *alto, tenor,* and *bass*

sostenuto: sustained, lengthened

sotto voce: in an undertone, i.e., quietly

spinto: a soprano or tenor voice that lies between lyric and dramatic in weight

stretto: tight, narrow; i.e., faster or hastening ahead; also, a passage in a fugue in which the contrapuntal texture is denser, with closely overlapping entries of the subject in different voices; by extension, similar closely imitative passages in other compositions

stringendo: tightening, narrowing; i.e., with a pressing forward or acceleration of the tempo; see also *stringendo*

subito: suddenly; e.g., *subito pp* instructs the player to suddenly drop to *pianissimo* as an effect

syncopation: a disturbance or interruption of the regular flow of downbeat rhythm with emphasis on the subdivision or upbeat

tacet: silent; do not play

tempo: time; i.e., the overall speed of a piece of music

tempo di marcia: march tempo

tenor: the second-lowest of the standard four voice ranges, generally extending from about the C below middle C to, in opera, the C above it; see also *soprano, alto,* and *bass*

tenuto: held; i.e., touch on a note slightly longer than usual, but without altering the note's value

tessitura: the pitch range; used to identify the most prominent or common vocal range within a piece of music

transition: a moment when, because or some block or barrier, an actor or singer has to change intention or find a new objective.

troppo: too much; e.g., *non troppo*, moderately or, when combined with other terms, not too much, such as *allegro [ma] non troppo* (fast [but] not too fast)

tutti: all; i.e., all together; usually seen in an orchestral or choral score when the orchestra or all of the voices come in at the same time

un poco più animato: a little more animated; i.e., play in a slightly more lively fashion

vibrato: vibrating; i.e., a more or less rapidly repeated slight alteration in the pitch of a note, used to give a richer sound and as a means of expression. Often confused with *tremolo*, which refers either to a similar variation in the volume of a note or to rapid repetition of a single note

vivace: very lively, up-tempo

vivacissimo: very lively

vocal score: see *piano-vocal score*

voce: voice

SUGGESTED READING

THEORY

The theater world is rich in theory—theory for acting, for staging, for social relevance, for sexual politics, for revolution. I like the basics. A list of books I have learned most from would include (in alphabetical order): John Barton, *Playing Shakespeare* (London, 1984); Richard Boleslavsky, *Acting: The First Six Lessons* (New York, 1949); Peter Brook, *The Empty Space* (London, 1968) and *The Open Door* (London, 1995); Toby Cole, *Directors on Directing: A Source Book of the Modern Theatre*, 2nd ed. (New York, 1963); Uta Hagen, with Haskel Frankel, *Respect for Acting* (New York, 1973); Robert Lewis, *Method—or Madness?* (New York, 1958); and Constantin Stanislavski, *An Actor Prepares*, trans. Elizabeth Reynolds Hapgood (New York, 1948). In addition, Wesley Balk has written two books specifically on acting in opera, *The Complete Singer-Actor: Training for the Music Theatre* (Minneapolis, 1992) and *Performing Power: A New Approach for the Singer-Actor* (Minneapolis, 1985); these go in a different direction than mine but have a devoted following.

HISTORY

There are many books on the history of opera. A good one is Leslie Orrey, *Opera: A Concise History*, revised and updated by Rodney Milnes (London, 1987). A more specialized but to me extremely useful history is Patrick Smith's study of libretti, pretty much from opera's beginnings: *The Tenth Muse: A Historical Study of the Opera Libretto* (New York, 1975). And then, for early opera, there is Ellen Rosand's *Opera in Seventeenth-Century Venice: The Creation of a Genre* (Berkeley, 1991). Or, for Italian opera, David Kimball's academic history, *Italian Opera* (Cambridge, 1994).

OPERAS

A general reference work of fundamental importance is *The New Grove*

Dictionary of Opera, ed. Stanley Sadie, 2nd ed. (London and New York, 1992). For specific operas, a wonderful resource is a series of guides published by John Calder for the English National Opera. Each book contains brief essays on a particular opera as well as a libretto in the opera's original language and a modern English translation. (Though some titles in the series have been out of print, all are now available using print-on-demand technology.) For this book we used the volume on the operas of Monteverdi.

For background on specific operas or composers we used a range of sources. For *L'incoronazione di Poppea*, the ENO book. For Rossini, Stendahl's *Life of Rossini*, trans. Richard N. Coe, rev. ed. (New York, 1970); see also Richard Osborne, ed., *Rossini: His Life and Works*, 2nd ed. (Oxford and New York, 2007). For *Faust*, the basic book is Stephen Huebner, *The Operas of Charles Gounod* (Oxford, 1990), but it is also important to read Christopher Marlowe's *Doctor Faustus* (there is a Penguin edition, ed. Frank Romany and Robert Lindsey, New York, 2003), as well as Edith Wharton's superb *The Age of Innocence* (London, 2006). A lot has been written about Handel as his operas have begun to come back into the mainstream over the last fifty years: see Donald Burrows, ed., *The Cambridge Companion to Handel* (Cambridge, 1997), and *Handel* (Oxford, 1994); Winton Dean, "The Performance of Recitative in Late Baroque Opera," in his *Essays on Opera* (Oxford, 1990), and the essential "Production Style in Handel's Operas," in Burrows, ed., *The Cambridge Companion to Handel* (Cambridge, 1997). For Donizetti, look at William Ashbrook's *Donizetti and His Operas* (Cambridge, 1982). And finally, for *Eugene Onegin*, there is of course Pushkin's extraordinary poem. It is available in several English translations; I have read the one by Charles Johnston for Penguin (London and New York, 2003). Tchaikovsky's letter about the composition of the opera is published in Modest Tchaikovsky, *The Life and Letters of Tchaikovsky*, vol. 1, ed. Rosa Newmarch (Viana House, 1973); musicological commentary is in John Warrack, program notes to Peter Tchaikovsky, *Eugen Onegin*, cond. James Levine (Deutsche Grammophon, 1988).